Woodturning
& DESIGN

To my wife Liz
for her total backing
and constant encouragement
ever since I became
interested in
turnery

Woodturning & DESIGN

RAY KEY

B.T. BATSFORD LTD, LONDON

© Ray Key 1985
First published 1985
Reprinted 1988

ISBN 0 7134 4115 1

Typeset by Latimer Trend & Company Ltd, Plymouth
and printed in Great Britain by
Anchor Brendon Ltd
Tiptree, Essex
for the publishers
B. T. Batsford Ltd.
4 Fitzhardinge Street
London W1H 0AH

Contents

List of colour plates 6
Acknowledgements 6

1 Slow developments 7
2 Earning a living *11*
3 Influences *15*
4 About lathes *23*
5 Machinery *28*
6 Turning tools *32*
7 Sharpening *38*
8 Chucks *41*
9 Other tools and accessories *47*
10 Helpful tips on techniques *50*
11 Finishing and finishes *54*
12 Timber buying and problems *60*
13 Domestic wares *68*
14 Designs for the home *70*
15 Individual objects *99*

Suppliers *142*
Index *143*

Colour plates

Between pages 72 and 73
Brazilian tulipwood box.
Boxes, left to right: olivewood, putumuju,
 birdseye maple.
Burr elm bowl.
Californian-grown English walnut dish.

Between pages 96 and 97
Quilted paldao platter.
Shaped cocobolo bowls and boxes.
Wet-turned natural-topped ripple pear bowls,
   with the log from which they were cut.
Natural-topped African blackwood bowl.
Natural-topped burr mulberry bowl.

Acknowledgements

I should like to thank all the craftsmen and
designers I have had the pleasure of meeting
and learning from over the years, especially
those mentioned in this book; Mark Wilkins
for help with some of the illustrations, the
lathe manufacturers for their information and
photographs; and also those woodturners who
have provided photographs of their work for
inclusion. The remaining photographs are by
the author, with the exception of Fig. 9
(Stone and Steccati); 14 and 15 (Rudi
Christl); 16 (Paul G. Beswick); 262 (photo-
graph and log supplied by Rolston Timber).

All work is by the author unless otherwise
credited.

1 Slow developments

Woodturning is one of the oldest crafts known to man, yet in some ways it is still a Cinderella, although the craft is practised by thousands. There are probably as many lathes as potters' wheels in garages and garden sheds up and down the country, but in the eye of the general public the craft has not yet become acceptable as most others have in the last fifteen to twenty years. Why is this?

Some blame can be attributed to the makers themselves, for much work lacks good craftsmanship and, most noticeably, good design. In addition, wood as a material seems to hold little mystery for the public. This can be attributed to the fact that it is all around us; we burn it, we build houses and fences, make furniture, paper, etc. from it. For all this, wood should be held in some reverence as the most versatile material in the world, yet it is as if familiarity breeds contempt. All this makes the life of any craftsman working in wood somewhat difficult; he is often met with a certain resistance to sales because of this attitude. This has been reinforced by the generally poor standard of woodturning on sale to the public. Many factors have contributed to this – Third World imports, for one, often selling at less than the price of the raw materials in England. The quality is frequently poor, but many a craftsman seems to try and compete by lowering his own standards, and therefore that of all woodturning in the public eye. Another factor is reliance on the use of mass-produced accessories, often of poor quality, which dominate the product rather than enhance it – for example, ceramic tiles set into a wood surround. It is the tile people buy, not the turned wood, as I know from my own experience in the long-distant past when the thought of selling dictated my taste (or lack of it). Yes, this work will sell, unfortunately. Yet accessories that do not dominate are perfectly acceptable if of good quality, where the design and the craftsmanship in wood produce a pleasing, useful item, such as a pepper mill, the knob only showing, or a table lamp with its brass fitting, the wood remaining the dominant factor throughout.

The main reason, though, to my mind, why there are not many quality turners around, is the lack of establishments that teach woodturning. It is not even taught as a subject in its own right; it is part of the general woodwork class. This is not the case with most other crafts; almost every school and technical college in the country runs day and evening classes in pottery, jewellery, weaving, etc. Not that this will necessarily produce thousands of potters, jewellers or weavers, but it will serve to give many an appreciation and insight into what it takes to create worthwhile products, and bring a realization that being a creative craftsman is not so easy. It will also prompt people, with their newfound insight, into purchasing the work of good craftsmen, promoting the craft's general acceptance. Yes, woodwork classes are also run, but most people wanting to learn turning will find things difficult. A question I am often asked is, 'Where can I get tuition at an evening class?'

The usual story is that there is a lathe at the evening school nearby but the teacher knows little about turning. There's the rub. If teachers are not given the necessary training it is impossible for them to teach their students; thus the development of the craft remains slow. There are, I know, some excellent teachers around, but they are often frustrated in their efforts, with a class of twenty or so and only one lathe. The result is often counter-productive, for to keep little Johnny happy while he waits his turn on the lathe, he may be asked to render a 50 mm (2 inch) square into an octagon by hand prior to mounting on the lathe, which is quite unnecessary. This may take him an hour or two, and then when his turn eventually comes, half an hour on the lathe may be all that is needed to achieve his aims. At the end of that he must have his doubts about turning.

The teacher is operating with severe restrictions, and any call for more equipment is likely to get a negative response from our educational overlords, for there are no Ordinary or Advanced level examinations in woodturning. In metalworking there are exams, and if results have been good the call for £4,000 or £5,000 spent on a new metal lathe may be granted. Five or six wood lathes could have been purchased with that sort of money.

So how do most would-be turners cope with these frustrations? Some, no doubt, give up because of the lack of tuition available at their nearby educational establishments. Most, however, become self-taught from books on the subject, but there can be no substitute for good tuition. Being able to ask questions on problems and receive instant answers on how to deal with them, if you grasp what you are told, will result in faster progress than battling away in the workshop with a book. Short courses are taken by many turners, and these can be very successful if the teaching is good. The problem that can arise, though, is that as such courses are rather intensive, some of what you thought you had grasped at the time is forgotten on returning to your workshop. If the teaching has been good and you have a good grasp of things, observing another turner at work or attending a seminar on the subject may shed some light on your problem. There is hope in some areas, however, as there are teachers who do seem to surmount many of these obstacles and manage to get their students to produce some worthwhile work.

When you have someone with the insight of Mr Hopkinson of Hanley Castle High School, preparing his class prior to a visit to West Midlands Arts 'Woodturning Today' Touring Exhibition in 1983 (put together by myself), we can all take heart. I quote from his notes to all pupils.

> This visit will provide you with an opportunity to widen your knowledge of timbers, and view in one exhibition the work of the finest woodturners in Britain today. You will be able to see the wide variety of ideas which these makers have put into their work. It is because they have been innovative in their ideals and highly skilled in the making, that they have reached the position which they now deservedly occupy.
>
> Notice how each woodturner endeavours to display the full beauty of the wood in his work; also note the simplicity of the design. Nothing appears complicated or awkward, the shapes or forms are subtle and elegant, some more than others, yet this simplicity of design is executed with such skill that the final product can create quite a powerful effect upon you.

This expresses many of my own feelings and thoughts, which will become abundantly clear later in this book. He continues:

> Only by recording the details of this exhibition can you hope to build up a reservoir of ideas, which you can then adapt (not copy, that's the point), for your own work.

He goes on to encourage students to undertake a project that has been inspired by their visit, to ask questions, observe and note names, timbers, tools, sketches, remember which item impressed them most, and so on. Let's hope there are soon many more teachers like him; I know of a few and am sure there must be others.

With the efforts of such teachers and the craftsmen themselves, there is no earthly reason why it should not be accepted that turners are capable of producing most desirable artefacts. If this is achieved, an overall higher standard and public acceptance will follow.

It may seem odd that there should be this need to try and establish the craft on a higher level, considering that it has been in existence for some 3,000 years, but for the greater part of its history woodturning has been used to produce utilitarian domestic utensils or components for works considered more worth while. This to some degree may explain some of the misgivings many people feel towards turnery. Most other crafts over the years have shown a much stronger development towards aesthetic or art-orientated forms. This gives rise to a much greater public and establishment appreciation, giving these crafts more status than ones producing just the utilitarian type of work, although these are of no less importance.

Through these developments a craft starts to assume a degree of recognition that was

1 Olivewood bowl 130 mm ($5\frac{1}{8}$ in) dia. × 85 mm ($3\frac{3}{8}$ in) high × $2\frac{1}{2}$ mm ($\frac{3}{32}$ in) thick, 1983.

2 Selection of boxes in exotics, 1984; left to right: Indian rosewood, Brazilian tulipwood, Mexican rosewood.

previously lacking. This allows those connected with it greater freedom of innovative development, and a chance to charge higher prices, provided the quality and design warrant this.

My comment about utilitarian-type work being no less important, I feel, is valid, for much work produced during the seventeenth and eighteenth centuries by the most accomplished of the English turners was of a quality and elegance that would be envied today.

This was mainly in the area of drinking vessels for the wealthy, made for the most part from lignum vitae. But even though wood in the turned form was much admired, desired and used, when an object of real value was required it was to gold, silver or ivory that the wealthy turned their attention – not much has changed. Another point to note is that, unlike many other craftsmen, no names of turners have gone down in history; the craft has always been the poor relation. A change in this direction is much overdue.

Turnery seems to have suffered a decline in quality during the nineteenth and certainly the first half of the twentieth century. However, since the late fifties standards have improved, due initially, I feel, to the Scandinavian influence with its clean, uncluttered lines.

It is interesting to note that when the revival of the craft began in earnest during the sixties and early seventies, turning lagged behind in development not only in Britain, but also in the USA. Now, however, there is a strong set of creative individuals in America who set out somewhat earlier than ourselves in trying to redress this balance.

Nevertheless, we now have several turners in the United Kingdom producing work of high quality, both in the domestic and aesthetic fields – but there is room for more at the top.

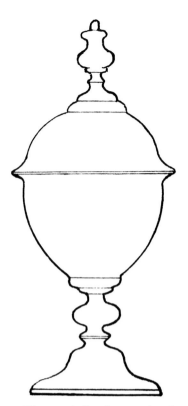

3 Elegant chalice from early 1600s.

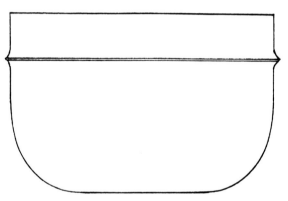

4 Wassail bowl modern in shape but seventeenth-century.

2 Earning a living

Earning a living from any craft is never going to be easy, nor will the financial rewards be high. If a new car each year, the latest electronic gadget, an ever changing wardrobe of clothes, or regular holidays are high on your list of requirements, don't become a craftsman.

Few craftsmen will ever be able to command an income to cater for these needs, even if they reach the top of their chosen craft. But it is possible, usually with a vast change of direction from the original ideals on which the hope of becoming a craftsman were founded.

This usually takes the course of employing others, mostly in a semi-skilled capacity. If it is pottery, by way of moulding and slip-casting. If turning, it is automatic copying lathes. Nothing remotely like the original intentions. Sometimes this is planned; with others it happens almost by accident, but once set on this path it is difficult to pull back. Often machinery has been purchased with the aid of a bank loan, and staff taken on, and there is pressure to do more of the same; to pay off the loan and keep paying the wages. The craftsman's original idea of earning a living with his hands, producing work of high quality with an individual stamp, has gone. The course I have described usually results in a semi-mass-produced product with the original maker never having time to make anything. He has become a businessman, salesman, works manager out of necessity, but the last thing he now is, is a craftsman. Such a set-up will often result in a greater income than could have been generated by remaining an original maker, but be warned; the worries of keeping a small workforce happy, keeping orders rolling in, justifying the purchase of new machinery, etc. will be greater than those of the man who has remained independent. If this is what you want then the best of luck, for you will need it.

Remember that the individual who is wondering if he has enough money for food next week can often go out and sell a few pieces, but the man with a workforce to pay needs to guarantee much larger sales.

Let's get back to what it takes to be a successful individual craftsman in this day and age. It is no good just being an excellent craftsman, you need to be much more. The ability to make must be backed with a sound understanding of the material you use and an ability to utilize its natural beauty by way of designs that will enhance it to the full. Being able to sell your work and yourself plays no small part. You must be an accountant, a businessman and professional in all your dealings. The need to show an integrity made up of high ideals, aims and objectives, will require a dedication that will result in the need to work long hours. Good health is a must for anyone thinking of being a craftsman. If you are married you will need the whole-hearted support of your wife or husband, for there are going to be many disappointments and problems along the way. Without Liz's belief, encouragement and total commitment I might never have become a turner, or might have ceased to have been one along the way. If you haven't this sort of backing it is going to be even more difficult to battle through. It all sounds rather daunting, doesn't it, for very few will possess all the above qualifications. This is perhaps why only a few make it to the top. Nonetheless there are a few thousand craftsmen around earning their living in a manner much as they prefer, but having to make more compromises than those who reach the top. Most are happy to do so. They prefer to do this rather than work for someone else.

Much of the foregoing warning is an attempt to dispel a myth that seems to have grown up around craftsmen. A visit to a country workshop in some idyllic setting on a summer's day often seems to conjure up a romantic notion that all a craftsman needs to do is turn up and all will be well with the world. In truth, he will put in longer hours, have less holidays, work harder and earn less than most of those visiting him. But he is probably much happier, for he is getting satisfaction from what he does at a time when fewer and fewer people are obtaining job satisfaction, in this mechanical computer age in which we live.

There are areas within each craft where it is possible to earn a living. In woodturning there are many possibilities open for choice: reproduction, antique restoration, architectural, domestic utilitarian, toys, games or the one-off aesthetic.

In my own case, the field chosen has been that of domestic and aesthetic turned items, for this is what I came out of industry to do. All other areas of turnery hold little interest for me. Reproducing the designs of others, producing balustrades for staircases, etc., are far too constraining and repetitive for my liking. That is not to say I haven't done these things on the odd occasion, but it's usually been done as a favour for a friend or a good customer.

If you specialize, you may well have more times when the work doesn't flow in, than the turner who is prepared to tackle almost every facet of the craft, in the earlier days, but if you are good enough and prepared to battle for what you really want to do, you should win through in the end, at the same time building a reputation for your work within the area where you have chosen to operate. Word of mouth – the bush telegraph – represents the best recommendation of any person's work.

If you are producing similar products in concept to my own, here are a few ways that you may like to consider selling your wares, for it is through selling your work that you are going to earn your living. My own approach has been consistent throughout, selling some 90 per cent of my work through craft shops and galleries, by way of direct purchase, not on sale or return, and also through exhibitions within galleries where invitations have been extended to show my work.

The other 10 per cent has been through our own retail shop run by my wife, or our local County Crafts Guild Exhibitions. If you choose to take this course, remember that most shops will mark up your work 100 per cent. This often puts craftsmen off, some feeling the retailer is cashing in on their expertise. This is seldom the case, for the operating costs of shops are high, especially as craft sales are still relatively low, despite their growth in recent years compared with other forms of merchandise.

Another approach is through direct sales to the public, via the workshop showroom (planners permitting), craft fairs, agricultural shows, etc. You will be able to charge more than if selling to a retailer, but you will need to, for while you are selling, you are not making. Many craftsmen like this contact with the public and market atmosphere, but for me the sight of thousands of faces, plus many a silly question at fairs and shows, holds very little appeal. If this is the way you like to sell, by all means do so, but another danger is that you will often be dealing with a far less demanding public than those that frequent the galleries. You are, therefore, more likely to settle for the ordinary, rather than strive for the constant improvement gallery owners and their clientele will demand.

Your overall goal must be constant improvement in both your craftsmanship and your designs. There is never a time for complacency. Looking back over my own work since 1973 when I first started earning my living from woodturning, I can see this constant improvement. There is much around that I would like to deny ever having made. Even today, many is the time, looking at an item made a few days earlier, when I think how it could have been improved. There is within me a strong perfectionist streak, driving me to try and improve all the time, learning from previous mistakes. However, if you do possess this driving force it is important not to let it get out of hand, for it can be a dangerous path to tread, becoming so inward-looking and self-critical that you never make anything you are

OPPOSITE ABOVE
5 Yew bowl, Mexican rosewood box, 1977.

OPPOSITE BELOW
6 Burr elm bowl, Indian ebony box, 1984. Similar shapes to those in Fig. 5 but more refined.

satisfied with. What you regard as perfect, is far from being so in another person's eyes. As the saying goes, 'beauty is in the eye of the beholder'. It can be a tortuous road to take, with little fulfilment or feeling of achievement if you take it too far. The answer must be to work to the best of your ability at all times. Most of us need a challenge to continue our improvements. In my own case this comes through exhibitions. Here there should always

7 The two boxes from Figs 5 and 6 together, showing the marked design improvement.

be a strong representation of the type of work your reputation has been built on, plus some new direction or development of ideas that has been lurking at the back of your mind for some time.

As you can see, a craftsman's life is never easy, but then nothing worth doing ever is.

3 Influences

We are all influenced by the things and people around us from an early age, some people more than others, and no doubt a great deal is in the subconscious. In my own case, my father led me into working with my hands. He was always building something, before the days of DIY. He trained as a shoemaker and later became a painter and decorator, working to his own high standards. All this no doubt influenced me.

When I was nine years old, an old schoolteacher of mine told my mother that I would never be an academic, but would always earn a living with my hands. So, at an early age, the course seemed set. Wood was the material even then that attracted me, fretwork and carving being the interest at that time. In my early teens, the school woodwork shop held a certain fascination and my first taste of woodturning occurred by way of making a wooden handle for a small garden fork made in the metalwork department. This was the compensation received, for I had no feeling for metal after the warmth of wood. By now, wood

was in my blood and I knew that was what I wanted to earn my living with.

On leaving school, I became a pattern maker, serving a five-year apprenticeship. During this time I learned a great deal, reading complicated drawings, making objects of great accuracy and learning the processes of casting and the production of many other products. A fair amount of turning was also undertaken as most of the men there hated it, but I suspect it was the old flat-belt lathe which must have come from the Ark that was the real reason. The turnery undertaken was nothing remotely like that I produce today; the items were all segmented and scraped into shape, not turned in the accepted form. A short time after completing my apprenticeship, fate dealt its hand. Redundancy came after a prolonged pattern makers' strike. If this hadn't happened I might still have been a pattern maker today – who knows?

Two years making moulds in wood and fibreglass followed, the latter a dreadful

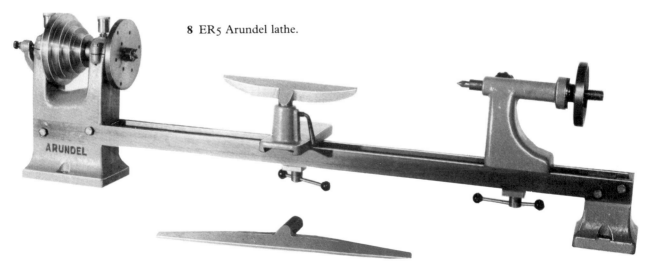

8 ER5 Arundel lathe.

9 Group of exotic bowls by Bob Stocksdale, 1984.

material for any wood-lover. During this time I
purchased my first lathe, about 1965, no doubt
suffering withdrawal symptoms from working
in fibreglass.

A move to another job and another material
followed. Clay, not the potter's variety, but the
type used in automobile styling studios
throughout the world. At this time I also met
my wife, who has proved to be the biggest
single influence in my life. Several things
started to happen around this time: the interest
in wood went unabated, and a greater insight
into design and the understanding of form was

acquired, working with the stylists who are
trained artists and designers. No doubt, on
reflection, a great deal of what I learned was
subconscious.

The need to work with wood was strong and
most evenings found me working on the lathe,
trying to learn the techniques needed to
become a successful turner from Fred Pain's
The Practical Woodturner. This was in the late
sixties when the craft revival was gathering
momentum. At weekends and holidays, visits
to craft shops and craftsmen were the order of
the day, looking for turners of quality.

There were three people at that time who
impressed me: George Sneed, whose work was
perhaps in advance of the public appreciation

at that time; John Trippas and Dennis French, both domestic woodware production turners. It was not necessarily the objects they produced, but the sheer consistency of their standard that impressed me most. Most people will make something worthwhile occasionally if they do enough of a thing, but it is being able to do it consistently that counts in the long run.

Long hours of practice and gradual improvement resulted, always aiming for the standards of the men I admired. In 1971, an exhibition of my work was arranged in a Warwick bookshop, all domestic woodware. This was more successful than we dared hope. Encouraged by this modest success, my wife opened a small craft shop later that same year, selling my work and other craft-related products.

Filled with the enjoyment of working with wood and the disenchantment of working in industry with its politics and bickering, with Liz's encouragement and blessing I decided in 1973 to try and make a full-time living from turnery.

We continued to look and learn, noting David Pye's fine boxes with admiration, and also the work of the Raffan brothers. In the mid-seventies, Richard, with his forceful sales approach, opened avenues for many others in retail outlets which had not really considered turned wood before.

Up to 1976, most of my work was domestic utilitarian in concept, mainly in teak and elm. Peter Dingley, the well-known gallery owner, encouraged me to use exotic timbers and produce work of a more aesthetic nature. This ultimately resulted in my acceptance on to the Crafts Council Index in 1977, followed by the offer of my first major exhibition by Angela and Stuart Houghton at Collection Gallery in Birmingham the same year, with some eighty items in twenty different timbers.

In 1979, a James Krenov Seminar at Parnham House saw my first meeting with Bob Stocksdale from USA, perhaps the world's best-known bowl turner. That meeting made a tremendous impression, possibly more than any other with a fellow woodturner, for he was using wood in a way not previously seen, and

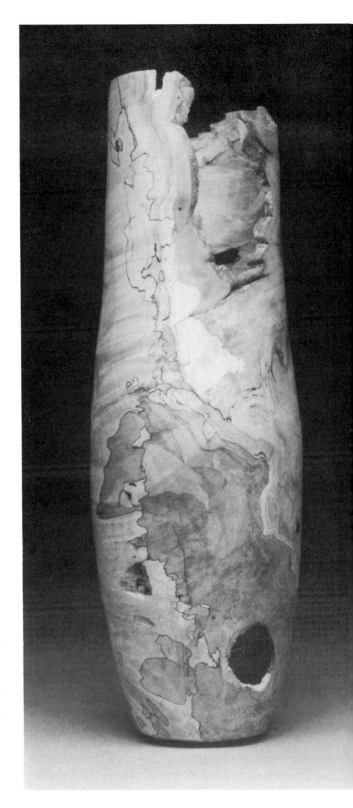

10 Spalted sugar maple 3 mm ($\frac{1}{8}$ in) thick, 445 mm (17$\frac{1}{2}$ in) high, 127 mm (5$\frac{1}{2}$ in) dia., by David Ellsworth, 1983.

11 Hollow redwood lace burl turning by David Ellsworth, 1983. Both 3 mm ($\frac{1}{8}$ in) thick; left: 355 mm (14 in) dia. × 203 mm (8 in) high. Right: 203 mm (8 in) dia. × 343 mm (13$\frac{1}{2}$ in) high.

had an understanding of the material's beauty in aesthetic forms with a delicacy normally associated only with fine porcelain.

In 1980, the International Woodturning Seminar was held at Parnham House. This provided another chance to meet Bob, and also David Ellsworth and Steven Hogbin. Their presentations and imaginations left me stimulated and awakened into looking at wood in a different way from any that had seemed

possible before. Everyone privileged to have been there must have gone away stimulated and questioning their own work. However, ultimately, one has to temper the desire to launch oneself heedless in their direction, as the UK market is far more conservative than that to be found in the USA. It is more often a question of timing when to try new ideas here, than the actual doing, if you want to eat.

In 1981 Dale Nish's second book appeared, with a wealth of photographs of turners' work which up to then I was unfamiliar with, but most showed an imagination and understanding of form not often seen in this country.

1981 also saw the Tenth Woodturning

12 Wormy ash bowl 254 mm (10 in) dia. × 63 mm (2½ in) high by Dale Nish, 1984. Sandblasted.

13 Wormy ash bowl 165 mm (6½ in) high × 140 mm (5½ in) dia. by Dale Nish, 1984. Sandblasted.

14 Turned chair by Stephen Hogbin, 1979.
Western red cedar, 863 mm (34 in) high.

15 Bowl by Stephen Hogbin, 1979. Australian walnut, 240 mm (9½ in) long.

Symposium in Philadelphia. It became a must to go when the list of names appeared, many of the best around: Ellsworth, Hogbin, Moulthrop, Stirt, Gilson, Mitchell, Stubbs, Linquist, Osolnik, Doyle, Nish, etc. It was like a *Who's Who* of woodturning, brought together by Al Le Coff. Key and Raffan were added to the list of demonstrator lectures once our interest was shown. The event proved a tremendous experience for all concerned because of the total commitment of the demonstrators to impart their knowledge and experiences to all attending. Most of those who

21

attended must have gone away inspired and some feeling dissatisfied with their own efforts, but all must have learned a great deal.

Accompanying the event was the Turned Object Show, with some one hundred exhibits, ranging from the bizarre to the superb, with the overriding theme of innovation and excellence. A few days' stay with David Ellsworth afterwards put the icing on the cake, and I spent time in his workshop and in general discussion into the early hours.

In 1982 Dale Nish, now a firm friend, visited our home for a few days. This provided me with a chance to gain greater insight into the American turnery scene and a few suggestions that have been most beneficial to my own work.

1983 provided a chance to meet many of the

16 'Ellipsoid bowl' by Ed Moulthrop, 1984. 990 mm (39 in) dia., tulipwood.

turners I have already named in San Francisco at a major wood show, plus the opportunity to visit the Stocksdales on their home ground, enjoying their company, and purchasing a bowl. None of this would or could have happened without the Nishes' invitation to their home, and the opportunity to lecture and demonstrate at Brigham Young University. Over the years, others have no doubt influenced me, but these have been the major factors.

The process of learning is never-ending and certain influences must filter through that spark off new ideas and thoughts.

4 About lathes

A question often asked by people interested in taking up turning as a hobby or a living is what lathe they should buy. It is not an easy question to answer, as a lot depends on the room a person has, how much he or she wants to spend and the type of work they want to undertake. In general, buy the best you can afford, as in everything else.

There are many lathes on the market today and it can become quite confusing with the claims and counter-claims of each manufacturer. Unfortunately, many are made with little thought for the person who is going to use them; it seems it is often a case of 'How easily and cheaply can we make them?' There are some that are almost certain to put off a would-be woodturner for life.

Bench-mounted machines are the most commonly produced lathes. With all of this type, mount them on a good solid wooden base; this will help absorb vibration. Don't use an old sideboard or prefabricated metal framework, but something like a good carpenter's bench. If you are right-handed it is always preferable to be able to turn on the inboard side of the headstock for face-plate work. Up until recent years you did not often find lathes that would allow diameters of more than 300 mm (12 in) to be turned in this way. In fact, most capacities were less. The most common way around this was a double-ended spindle allowing much larger diameters to be turned on the outboard end. This works, but it does mean you have to turn in a left-handed manner. When you first start learning to turn the less problems you encounter the better. For this reason, the lathes selected for illustration all enable you to work right-handed.

Tyme Avon

One of the newest machines on the market. Moderately priced, single-ended spindle with pivoting headstock through 180°, allowing you to work right-handed. At 90°, work up to 407 mm (18 in) diameter can be tackled; at 180°, 530 mm (21 in). The machine is supplied motorized but with only drive centre and tail centre. All other accessories are purchased separately. This gives the customer the complete choice, allowing him to purchase only what he considers necessary.

Arundel Treebridge K600

Another new lathe, from a proven maker, again moderately priced. Single-ended spindle, but in this case the headstock slides along the bed to the tailstock end to allow larger diameters to be tackled, in this case 559 mm (22 in). This lathe is supplied without any accessories, giving the customer freedom of choice.

Coronet Major

This lathe has been produced for many years. Again there is the pivoting headstock for right-hand operations, and 584 mm (23 in) diameter can be tackled. This lathe is supplied with several pieces of equipment, in contrast to the others.

All these lathes are similar in price, allowing for the cost of attachments and accessories, etc., so you pay your money and make your choice. It is best to view the maximum capacities of these machines for occasional use. If you plan to work in large diameters regularly then buy a heavy-duty lathe.

In the area of lathes which interests turners earning a living or the very serious, there are still many that are poorly designed. Many manufacturers produce poor tool rests, tailstock release handles, etc., while some even still go for spanner release. It is just not good enough. There are others that are solidly constructed in the headstock and bed area but are then mounted on flimsy, fabricated metal carbinates that rattle and vibrate.

However, there is one lathe that is head and shoulders above the rest for sheer quality.

Harrison Graduate lathe, short bed or long bed

This possesses the qualities needed in a lathe for use every day, and has a tremendously heavy cast headstock with excellent bearings, tool rest, quick-action release handles and excellent tailstock. For a serious bowl turner the short bed is a must. If spindle work is your major activity then you need the long bed.

Having owned a short bed since 1975, I view this as my best investment in machinery. A diameter of 496 mm (19½ in) can be turned on

17 Tyme Avon. Available in three centre lengths: 610 mm (24 in), 910 mm (36 in), 1,220 mm (48 in); 280 mm (11 in) swing over the bed; 200 mm (8 in) swing over tool-rest bracket; 500 mm (19½ in) diameter capacity at 90°; 580 mm (23 in) diameter capacity at 180°; ¾ hp single-phase motor; four-speed Poly-'V' drive 470, 750, 1,150, 2,000 r.p.m.; no. 2 morse taper head- and tailstock; hollow tailstock; tailstock and drive centres 253 mm (10 in) rest as standard. All other accessories as extras.

OPPOSITE ABOVE
18 Arundel K600. Available in two centre lengths: 914 mm (36 in); 1,219 mm (48 in); 228 mm (9 in) swing over bed; 559 mm (22 in) swing over the bench; ¾ hp single-phase motor; seven-speed Poly-'V' drive 375, 560, 690, 1,050, 1,200, 1,800, 2,200 r.p.m.; no. 1 morse taper head- and tailstocks; hollow tailstocks. All accessories extra.

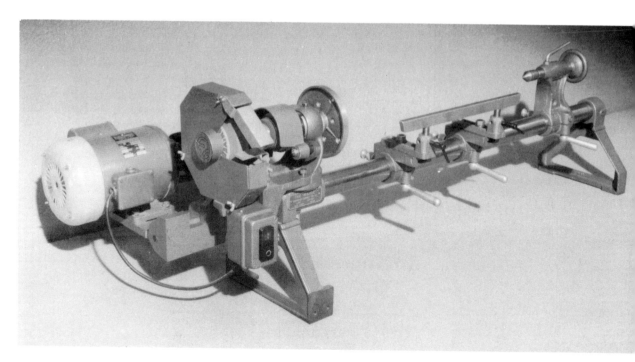

19 Coronet Major CMB 600. Between-centre capacity 838 mm (33 in); 228 mm (9 in) swing over the bed; 584 mm (23 in) capacity with headstock rotated; ¾ hp single-phase motor; five-speed Poly-'V' drive; no. 1 morse taper head- and tailstock; 175 mm (7 in) grindstone; 152 mm (6 in) face plate; four-prong drive centre; revolving tail centre; 431 mm (17 in) tool rest. All as standard.

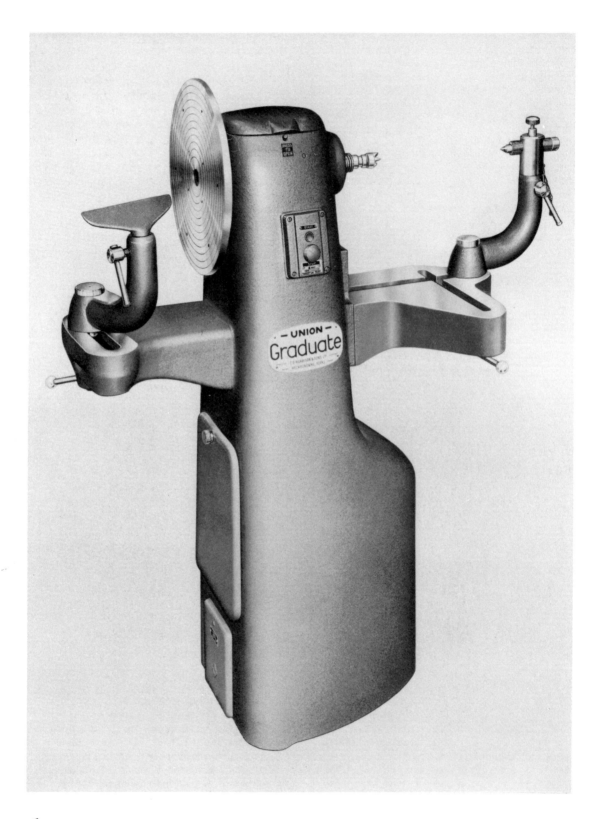

20 Harrison Graduate short bed. Between-centre length capacity: 400 mm (15¾ in); 356 mm (14 in) between-centre swing; 495 mm (19½ in) bowl capacity swing over the bed; 508 mm (20 in) outboard swing; 152 mm (6 in) deep 457 mm (18 in) dia.; 305 mm (12 in) deep 356 mm (14 in) dia.; ¾ hp single or three-phase motor; four speeds: 425, 790, 1,330, 2,250 r.p.m.; no. 3 morse taper headstock, no. 2 morse taper tailstock; hollow spindle; 356 mm (14 in) outer face plate, 203 mm (8 in) inner face plate; 356 mm (14 in) tee rest, 191 mm (7½ in) tee rest; cone, fork, cup centres. All as standard. Weight 3¾ cwt.

the inboard, 508 mm (20 in) on the outboard. A platter of 825 mm (32½ in) was once turned on mine with the arm removed for a tripod rest. A 1370 mm (54 in) capacity bed was purchased at a later date and is fitted when the need arises, but most of the time it is used as a short bed. Supplied with rests, face plates and centres, the price is about double that of the bench lathes, but the quality is superb. There is not another lathe in its class to compare. It will last a lifetime, with the odd bearing and belt replacement along the way.

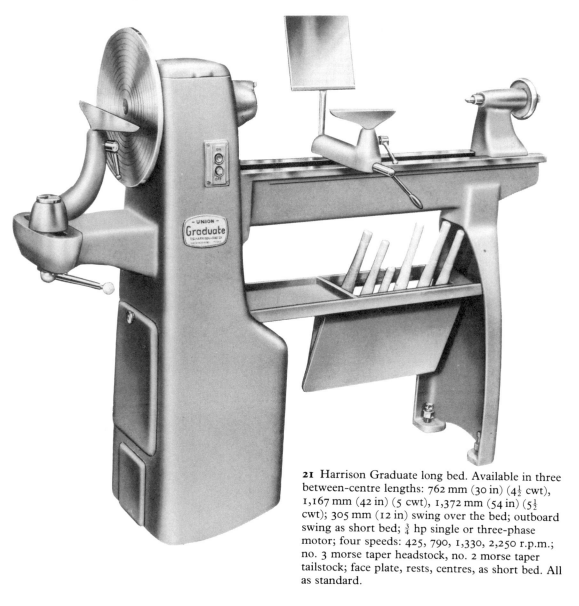

21 Harrison Graduate long bed. Available in three between-centre lengths: 762 mm (30 in) (4½ cwt), 1,167 mm (42 in) (5 cwt), 1,372 mm (54 in) (5½ cwt); 305 mm (12 in) swing over the bed; outboard swing as short bed; ¾ hp single or three-phase motor; four speeds: 425, 790, 1,330, 2,250 r.p.m.; no. 3 morse taper headstock, no. 2 morse taper tailstock; face plate, rests, centres, as short bed. All as standard.

5 Machinery

Having discussed lathes, let's move on to other items of equipment that make a turner's life easier. Let me first tell you what I have myself, then make comments afterwards: floor-standing band saw, pillar drill, bench grinder, disc sander, circular saw, router, dust extractor and electric drill. Of these, I would be quite happy to operate without the router and circular saw, both non-essentials for the wood turner. The others all have their place, and top priority would go to the band saw and bench grinder, closely followed by dust extractor, pillar drill and sanding disc.

If you are earning a living from turning, then all machines should be independent, not the multi-purpose variety. The cost is higher but the saving in time and frustration of swapping belts, unbolting attachments, etc., will be well worth the extra investment. When buying machinery, always buy the best you can afford, and usually something larger than you need at the time, for as you progress you will find it has been a wise move. I remember making do with a $\frac{1}{2}$ hp three-wheel band saw for some years; it proved to be a false economy, with constant blade breakages, lack of power, and poor tracking and guides. After I purchased a two-wheel floor-standing machine with a $1\frac{1}{2}$ hp single phase motor, $9\frac{1}{2}$ in depth of cut with fingertip adjustments, blade guides, etc., the folly of using the previous saw became instantly apparent. In fact, I began to wonder how I had managed at all. We all do it, but it is never worth while. The frustration and loss of time is immense.

Most things can be cut without trouble now, especially when a four-skip flexi-back blade is fitted. When timber larger than the saw's

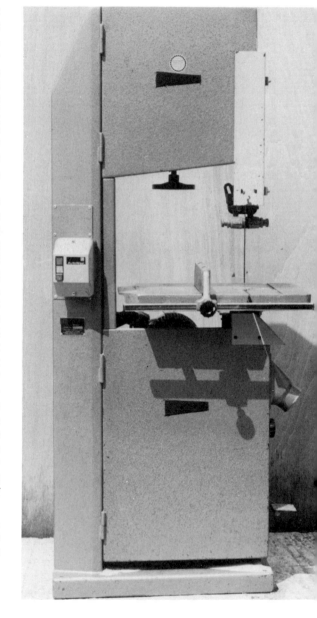

22 Band saw 400 mm throat ($15\frac{3}{4}$ in), 240 mm ($9\frac{1}{2}$ in) depth of cut.

23 178 mm (7 in) bench grinder.

capability needs cutting, then a chain saw becomes necessary. More on this later.

A double-ended bench grinder is a must. Do not buy smaller than a 6 in, and make sure there is plenty of power in the machine, and normal carborundum wheels of 36 grit for reshaping and removing deep nicks in tools at one end, and 60 grit for normal sharpening the other.

In my view the next machine needed is a dust extractor, especially if you use exotic imported and kiln-dried woods a great deal. And dust is the operative word. Don't worry about the shavings. It is those fine particles of dust that cause problems. For six years I worked using face masks, feeling this was an adequate precaution, and did not worry too much. I became increasingly aware of breathing difficulties, particularly when playing sport or any other form of physical exercise, but with the installation of a good dust extractor the problem was quickly resolved.

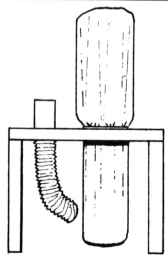

24 Effective dust extractor with 2 hp motor.

The dust extractor installed has a 2 hp single-phase motor, with a 16 in impeller blade, 7 in inlet from the ducting, a return air filter bag and a dust/shavings collection sack.

29

25 Lathe dust extractor hopper hood.

This is ducted to the lathe, band saw and sanding disc, with baffles in the ducting to give optimum suction to each machine. Lathes are not the easiest machines to collect dust from, but excellent results can be obtained using a PVC rainwater hopper head attached to a flexible tubing connected into the ducting. Adjustment in position to suit different diameters of work being turned is by string and wire, not very refined, but it works wonderfully. The manufacturer would have supplied a hopper head in sheet metal, virtually identical to my PVC one, for £120. Mine cost £3 for the same results.

Other methods that will deal with the dust problem, although not as effectively, are these. An extractor fan fitted in the wall or window behind the lathe, which is fine in summer but will take the heat out in the winter. An old vacuum-cleaner fitted close enough to the lathe gives limited success. Another possibility is the helmet type with built-in fan. I know people who swear by them, but for constant use they are somewhat cumbersome.

Other machines that I feel are of great benefit are the pillar drill, belt sander and sanding disc. You can do without both if turning is just a hobby, as you can drill on a lathe, and glue a sanding disc to a face plate in order to sand, but it is much easier and better to have independent machines designed for a specific purpose, as time and effort will be saved.

The electric hand drill also plays a big part in my workshop, as it is used a great deal in sanding face-plate work. More on that in the finishing section.

Another machine mentioned briefly was the chain saw. This is something I have managed without, up to now, choosing to hire one when the need arose. However, it can be an absolute must if you buy large trees uncut or make large items, or turn in wet wood. More on this later. You will also be surprised by how many times the offer of an odd tree comes your way, when people know you are a woodturner. If you have a chain saw you can deal quickly and effectively with the offer.

26 Pillar drill.

6 Turning tools

These break down into three major categories, each covering some variations. Major changes and development have taken place in turning tools in recent years with the use of 'high-speed' steel. Most tools made of this material have an 18 per cent tungsten content. This has made the forged gouges of yesteryear obsolete, at least for the professional.

Most of my own tools are now of that variety, and the rest will be replaced when and if they are available from the manufacturers. At first they may appear expensive, but the time saved in sharpening is immense, and the tools pay for themselves time after time, if you are earning your living from turnery.

Gouges

These are used in both forms of turnery, face-plate and spindle, but their angles and forms are often very different. For spindle work, roughing gouges with square ends ground around 45° are needed for reducing a square

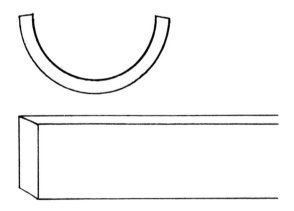

27 31 mm (1¼ in) roughing gouge, reduces squares to cylinders in seconds between centres 45° angle.

28 Typical between-centre spindle gouge, 30° angle.

section stock to a cylinder in double-quick time. For curves and grooves, fingernail shapes are the normal forms, with angles of 30° or so. These are normally available in standard and long and strong strengths. What is normally meant by these terms, is that standard strength refers to gouges with a constant metal thickness, whereas long and strong, as the term implies, are longer and metal thickness is much heavier in the base of the radius. A wide range of sizes of all these tools is generally available.

Bowl gouges

Bowl gouges have a much deeper U-shaped section, ground square across, with an angle of around 45°, in general. My own are all ground far more obtusely, around 60°–65°. Some are also the fingernail-shaped variety. The reasons for these adaptions are explained more fully in the chapter on techniques.

Skew and square chisels

These are the tools most people have the greatest difficulty in mastering, for if you do something wrong they let you know more quickly than any other tool. I remember being

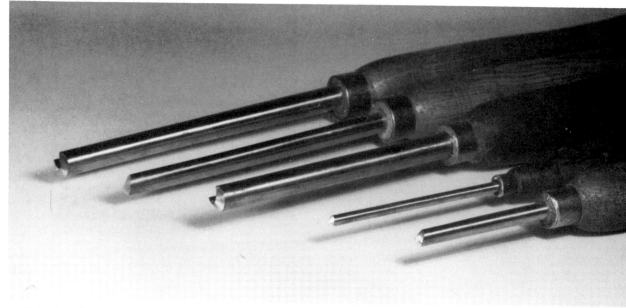

29 Selection of gouges.

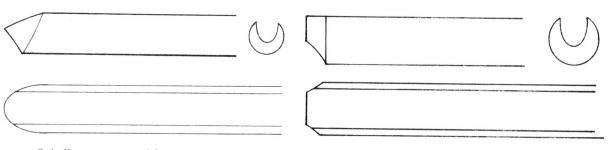

30 Spindle gouge ground for bowl use, 60°–65° angle.

31 Normal long and strong bowl gouge with 45° angle.

thanked for a lecture once by an amateur turner who picked up my skew chisel and described it as the Devil's own creation. He said that before becoming a Methodist he used to swear and curse it. He now quoted passages of the Bible at it, and his results were still the same.

Used correctly, chisels are perhaps the most versatile tool of all and capable of producing the cleanest surface results; they are used only in spindle turning. The use of skew or square-end often depends on the turner's preference or the work being undertaken. As a general rule, the skew has a cutting edge of 60°–70° with a bevel ground on both sides between 40° and 50°.

32 Long and strong bowl gouge ground to my preferred 60°–65° angle. All gouges high-speed steel.

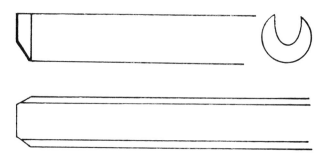

33

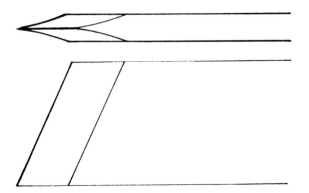

33 Skew chisel 60°–70° angle, bevel ground 40°–50° angle.

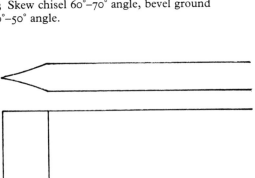

34 Square chisel, bevel ground 40°–50° angle.

This also goes for the square end. They are normally straight across on their leading edge, but I prefer them to have a convex form.

Gouges and chisels should all be ground slightly concave. This will happen automatically if you grind on the edge of the wheel, as you should.

Parting tools

At times these can act as small chisels for forming small beads, but their main function, as their names implies, is to part wood from the lathe. There are now several styles and sizes available. Four are described here.

3 mm (⅛ in) high-speed steel
Used to minimize mismatch of grain in boxes, etc. when removing the lid from the body.

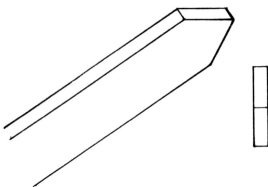

35 3 mm (⅛ in) high-speed steel parting tool used for small items and material-saving.

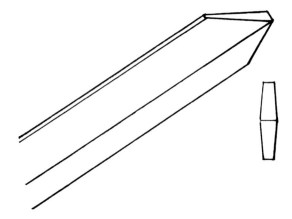

36 5 mm (³⁄₁₆ in) high-speed steel diamond parting tool, perhaps the most versatile, has good clearance.

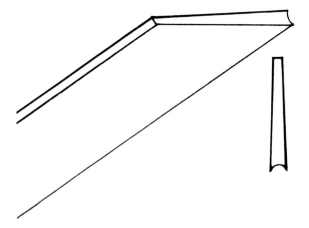

37 5 mm (³⁄₁₆ in) high-speed steel fluted parting tool, gives excellent finish used with the flute down, but can mark the tool rest.

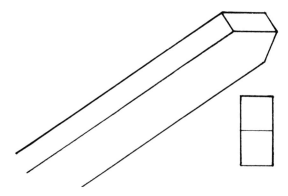

38 9 mm ($\frac{3}{8}$ in) beading or parting tool, can be used with the sizing tool.

5 mm($\frac{3}{16}$ in) high-speed steel
Diamond sections type; this is possibly the best all-round tool, giving good clearance when parting deep.

5 mm($\frac{3}{16}$ in) fluted high-speed steel
Gives a good finish, used with the flute downwards on the rest. The drawback of this tool is that it tends to put small nicks in the tool rest if used much; not good if you use a skew chisel a lot. I tend to limit its use to forming small beads on boxes, seldom using it as intended.

9 mm ($\frac{3}{8}$ in) beading/parting
Ideal tool for forming beads and spigots, as its width gives good bearing on the rest. Used in conjunction with a sizing tool, it also allows you to cut dowel and spigots on stool legs, etc., once set, without the need for calipers.

Scrapers

These are available in many forms, shapes and sizes. They are made from both carbon and high-speed steel of flat section, in standard and heavy weights. Standard are usually 5 mm/6 mm ($\frac{3}{16}/\frac{1}{4}$ in) thick while the heavy type are 9 mm ($\frac{3}{8}$ in) thick, and are used in larger work or when tool is cutting some distance from the rest, as their extra thickness gives added strength and serves to damp down vibration. This is the one tool in turnery where the bevel does not rub the work, being tilted slightly downwards, allowing the burr from the grindstone to remove shavings rather than dust. (If you get dust, resharpen, for torn or rough finishes will result from a blunt tool.) Angles are obtuse against other lathe tools, my own varying from as little as 15° to 25°.

39 Selection of scrapers.

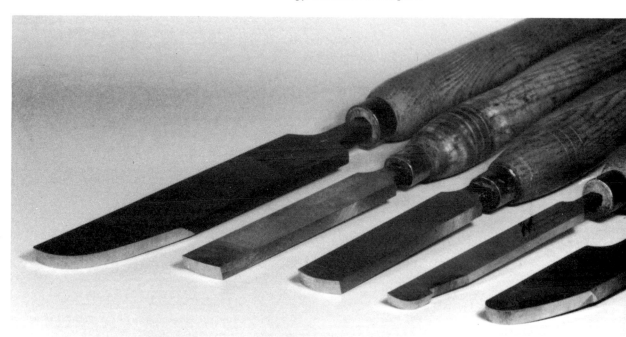

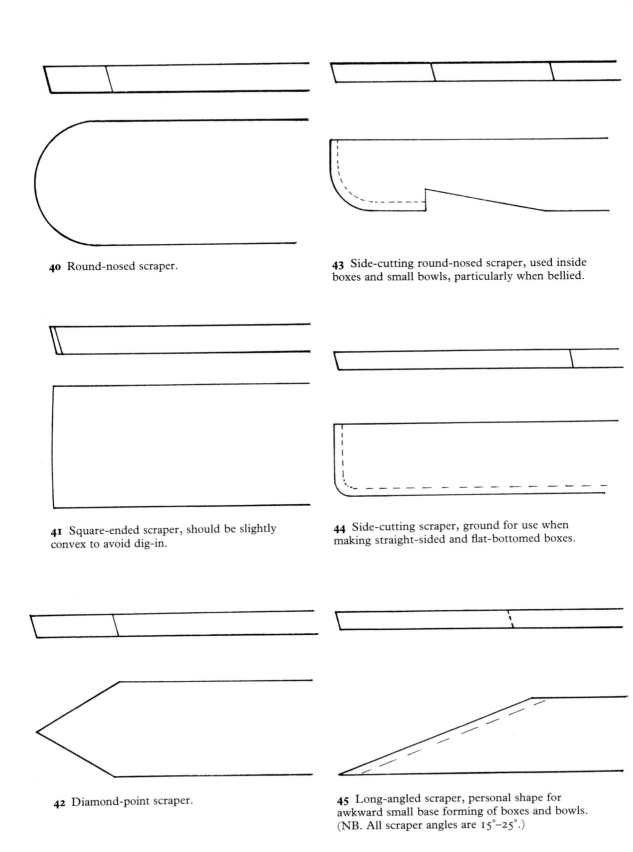

40 Round-nosed scraper.

43 Side-cutting round-nosed scraper, used inside boxes and small bowls, particularly when bellied.

41 Square-ended scraper, should be slightly convex to avoid dig-in.

44 Side-cutting scraper, ground for use when making straight-sided and flat-bottomed boxes.

42 Diamond-point scraper.

45 Long-angled scraper, personal shape for awkward small base forming of boxes and bowls. (NB. All scraper angles are 15°–25°.)

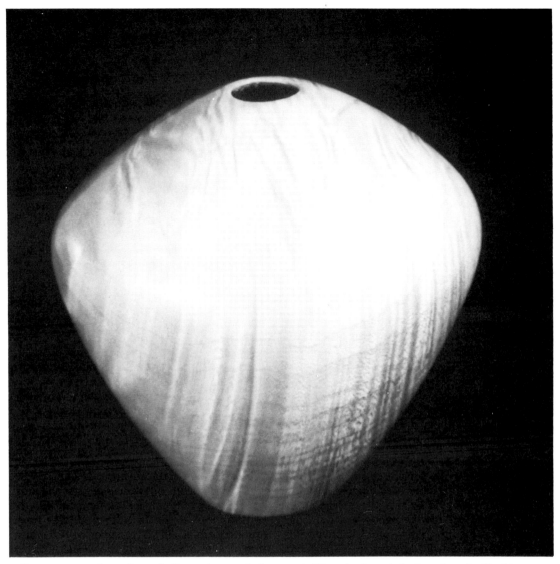

Scrapers are the safest of all turning tools in use and it is possible to make objects from start to finish with them. The results are slow, however, and the end-product rarely has the crispness obtained using true cutting tools. My own view of them is that they have no part to play in spindle turning at all, as it should be possible to use gouges and chisels throughout. For face-plate work they have a place, but do limit this, for it should be possible to create 90–95 per cent of all face-plate objects with gouges. The scraper should be limited to

46 Silver-leaf maple hollow form by David Ellsworth, 1981. Entrance hole 16 mm ($\frac{5}{8}$ in), constant wall thickness less than 3 mm ($\frac{1}{8}$ in).

removing ripples and undulations, and reaching areas that have proved impossible to reach with a gouge. There are exceptions to this general rule where great accuracy is required, for example pattern making, or making objects of the Ellsworth type, hollowing interiors through extremely small orifices.

37

7 Sharpening

The reader may feel that I have rather a cavalier approach to this area, and in some ways this is so, when you consider that whole books have been written on this subject alone.

My only real concern is that the tools are sharp and will carry out the job they are intended for. Angles of bevels are not of paramount importance to me, whereas others may feel if an angle is not exactly as described in some publication or another it becomes almost impossible to use that tool, and spend a great deal of time trying to achieve these aims.

Of course, certain angles do help, and the degree of variance permissible is less with chisels and spindle gouges, but they are not critical, for by lowering and raising the tool handle you compensate for any variation from your desired aim, thus still allowing the bevel to rub.

All my tools are ground on carborundum grinding wheels: 36 grit for major tool modification, 60 grit for finish-sharpening.

47 Grinding of a bowl gouge.

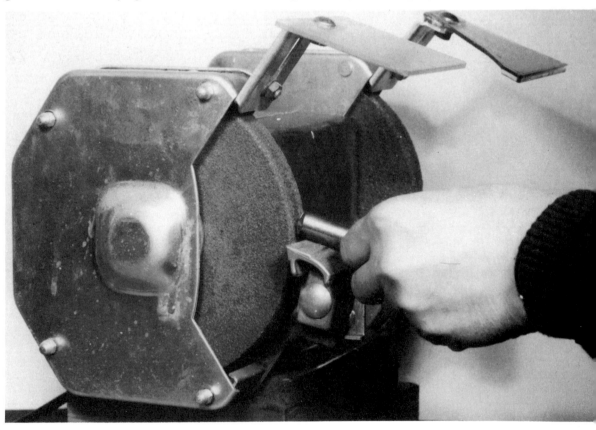

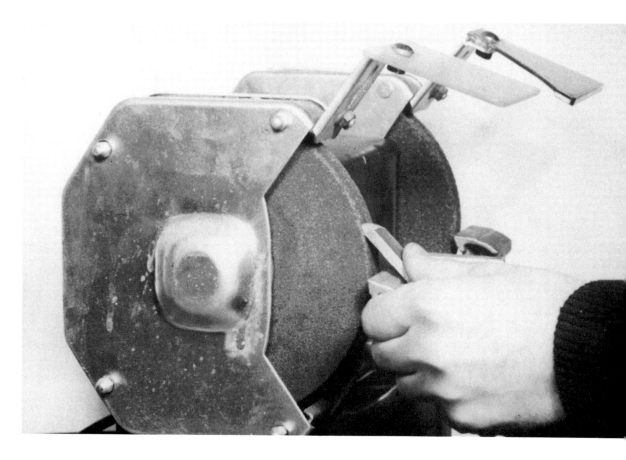

48 Grinding of a chisel.

Oil- and slip-stones have no place in my sharpening process. It is from lathe to grinder and back again as quickly and efficiently as possible. Turning is carried out on a lathe, not a grinder, and all tools are ground concave on the edge of the wheel, not the side. Convex and faceted bevels make tools almost impossible to use, and should be avoided at all times. When presenting a tool to the wheel, it will be found best to let the heel touch first, then lift the handle, allowing the edge to make contact. If sharpening a gouge, keep the heel and edge in constant contact with the stone, and rotate from top edge to top edge. Having been ground all the way round, the cutting edge should now be sharp again. With chisels, move them across the wheel from side to side with heel and edge in constant contact, not letting them become stationary, as this allows heat build-up which leads to blueing and subsequent softening of

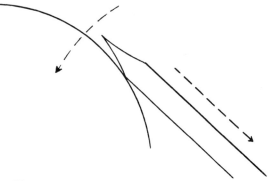

49 Heel of chisel makes contact with the grinding wheel first.

steel, causing tools to blunt far more quickly. There is usually a wire edge formed on chisels as they are ground from both sides, and it is normal procedure to oil-stone this off, but I choose to drag it through a soft block of wood; this does the trick and saves stoning. Scrapers rely on the burr created from the grinder to cut,

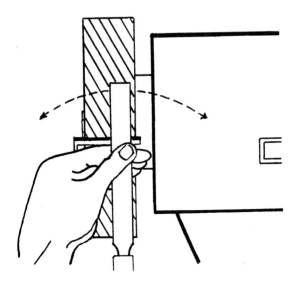

50 Grinding pivot movement.

so the last thing you need is an oil-stone.

One tip worth remembering is to keep all tools constantly on the move when in contact with a carborundum wheel; this will help minimize overheating, which results in softening of the steel. Keep water close by to cool tools in.

Much of the above may shock you but I can assure you that these methods work; also, with the use of high-speed steel which is less sensitive than carbon, the results are even better.

NB. Although my approach to the sharpening of tools may be somewhat cavalier, the same does not apply to safety precautions. Grinding wheels should always be used with the manufacturer's eye protection shields in place. If you use a grinding wheel without shields, use goggles to protect your eyes, for just one spark can cause a very serious eye injury. It is not worth the risk of neglecting eye safety precautions. While I am on the subject of safety, the use of old files to make scrapers is not to be recommended, for they are often brittle and can snap easily. Please buy good tools that are designed for the job of woodturning – it's far better to be safe than sorry.

8 Chucks

This is an area where significant developments have taken place in recent years, and there are now a number of excellent chucks on the market. The days of green baize, cork and labels to cover face-plate screw holes can and should be a thing of the past, if you are prepared to spend some money. First, let us look at the traditional chucks.

Face plate

Traditionally the favourite method of mounting wood on any lathe for headstock turnery. This role will no doubt diminish somewhat with the use of new mounting methods, but it will always have a significant

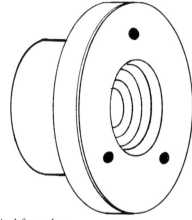

52 Typical face plate.

51 Selection of more traditional headstock fixing chucks.

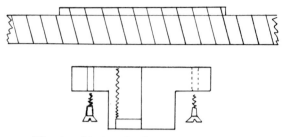

53 Wooden friction chuck.

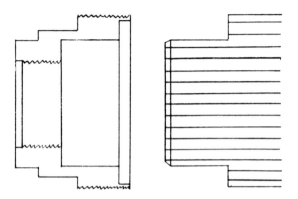

54 Cup chuck.

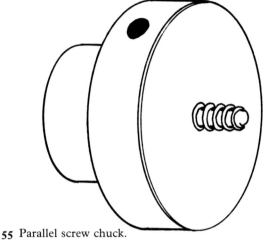

55 Parallel screw chuck.

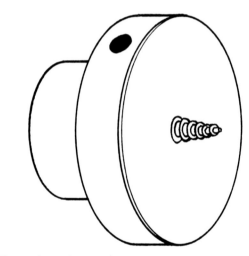

56 Tapered wood screw chuck.

part to play in most turners' workshops. It can be used as a back plate for many other methods of holding wood in the lathe other than with screws, once a waste block has been attached. These include spigot friction fit, glued newspaper joints, contact adhesives, and even double-sided tape direct to the face plate and base of the item. They all work, but must be viewed with reservation, for a dig in with a tool (catching a crab) will more often than not result in the work flying from the lathe.

Cup or bell chuck

This is another old favourite of many turners, although it is one I seldom use; it largely depends on the type of work you produce. Very useful for making items such as scoops, etc., but it is rather wasteful on timber.

Screw chuck

An old and trusted favourite which has been altered in recent years to the benefit of everyone. A parallel-machined screw is now

the order of the day. There are several makes available, all excellent, with slight variations of thread. The old tapered wood screw is a thing of the past. The main benefit of the parallel screw is that work can be removed from the lathe and remounted accurately every time. This was almost impossible with the old tapered type. The one thing to have in mind, though, is that a pilot hole must be drilled compatible to the size of screw, i.e. a 9 mm ($\frac{3}{8}$ in) parallel screw needs a 6 mm ($\frac{1}{4}$ in) pilot hole. The old tapered ones would pull on to almost any small pilot hole.

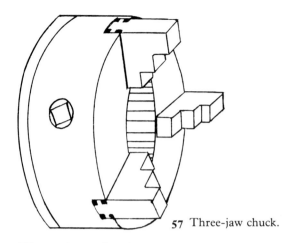

57 Three-jaw chuck.

Three-jaw chuck

This provokes more comment than any other chuck, because many people feel it is dangerous. Well, of course, it can be, but it is one I shall never do without, and since 1975 I suspect some 50 per cent of my work has been produced on one. They are expensive but last for years, if you buy a good one. They are fast-acting, self-centring on the work to be held, and I use them mainly for producing my boxes, bowls and platters. With the new breed of accurate chucks now available, the use of this chuck has been lessened a little, but it is still very important to me.

There have been many new chucks on the market in recent years, all having their uses but most with limitations. There have been collet, ring, coil grip, six-in-one, to mention just a few. But there are two that stand out head and shoulders above all others in my view: the precision spigot and the precision combination.

Precision spigot

This is used for gripping the base of small bowls, shallow dishes, etc.; for example 203 mm (8 in) bowls can easily be turned on a 38 mm ($1\frac{1}{2}$ in) diameter spigot of a 3 mm ($\frac{1}{8}$ in) length, and smaller bowls on the 25 mm (1 in) spigot work equally well, making it possible to incorporate the spigot form into a decorative feature of their base. Care must be taken not to overtighten, as it is possible to pinch small bases from bowls on cross-grained timber; on end grain this is impossible. Turning boxes on this sort of chuck keeps timber waste to an absolute minimum, just 3 mm ($\frac{1}{8}$ in), important when using exotics. My estimate is that the saving from a year's production enables me to produce another 35 to 40 boxes from what would otherwise have been shavings.

58 Selection of more recently produced headstock chucks.

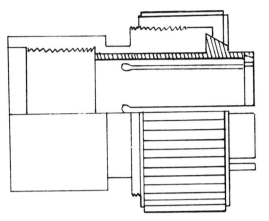

59 38 mm ($1\frac{1}{2}$ in) spigot chuck.

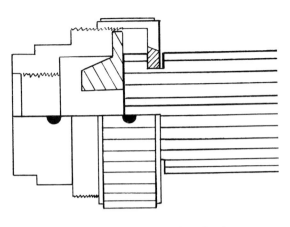

62 Precision combination split ring chuck.

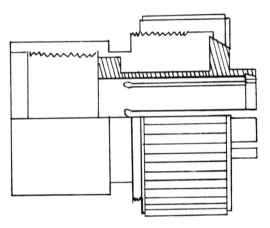

60 25 mm (1 in) spigot chuck.

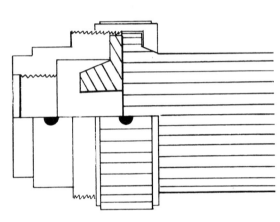

63 Precision combination ring chuck.

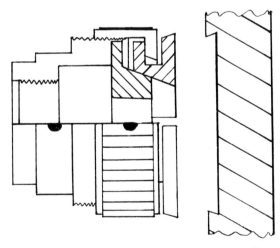

61 Precision combination chuck, expanding collet.

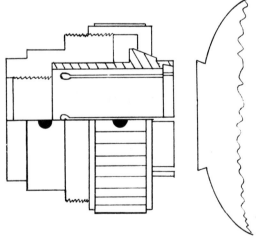

64 Precision combination 52 mm (2 in) spigot, 48 mm ($1\frac{7}{8}$ in) collet.

Precision combination

This is what its name claims: a precision combination. Certainly the best chuck ever produced, capable of many uses without losing accuracy. Not being a lover of multi-purpose combinations, universal (call them what you will) chucks or machines, I tend to be hard to please, but this chuck wins hands down; it is as good or better than most that are designed for independent use.

What are its uses? Well, it can be used in its basic form as an expanding collet, split ring, pin chuck, cup chuck and ring chuck. Extras make it a screw, 50 mm (2 in) spigot or 48 mm ($1\frac{7}{8}$ in) collet, all very useful. There is also a collet/spigot arrangement in similar size to the independent spigot. This is the one facet that isn't as successful as the independent, not because it does not grip well, but because the chuck's body is much larger than the independent, and limits access from behind when turning small items. Anyone thinking of buying a chuck should put this at the top of their list.

Pin chuck

Extremely useful for producing items from salt and pepper shakers to natural-topped bowls.

Face-plate rings

Cheap and effective way of mounting work on a three-jaw or precision combination chuck; allows work to be removed and remounted quickly. When faced with turning the outside of bowls and platters that are too large for screw- or pin-chucking in quantities, this is the answer. Also ideal for the classroom, where all

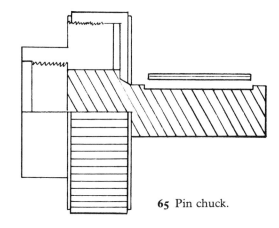

65 Pin chuck.

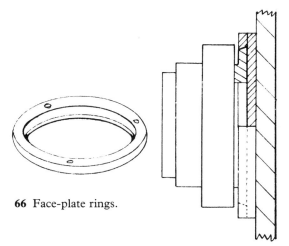

66 Face-plate rings.

pupils can mount a face-plate ring and be ready to use the lathe immediately without the delay of removing a face plate from the previous work.

67 Selection of between-centre drive chucks.

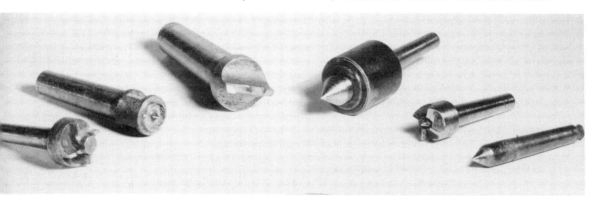

45

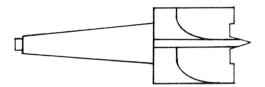

68 Four-prong drive centre.

69 Cone centre.

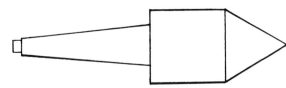

70 Revolving centre.

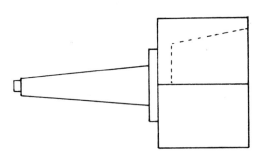

71 Headstock conical friction chuck.

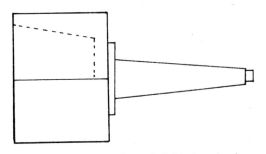

72 Revolving tailstock conical friction chuck.

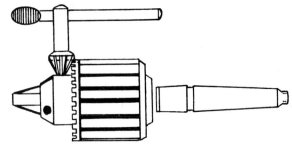

73 Jacobs chuck.

All this relates to chucks for headstock, faceplate turnery. No mention of between-centre work at all. It is an area that by and large doesn't need these refinements, as the work mounted is between centres and it is largely a matter of preference. At the headstock end, you use a two- or four-pronged centre and at the tailstock end a cone, ring or revolving. My own preference is for a hardened four-prong, with the tailstock a high-quality revolving one. Emphasis on quality for the revolving one is high, for problems here will magnify when working; all have morse taper shaft. There has been one development in chuck form for between-centre work. This is the conical friction drive chuck.

Conical friction chuck

Useful to those who want to product split turning work, small patterns, reproduction and antique restoration, although rather an expensive way of achieving these aims. If this is your line of work then no doubt the chucks will soon pay for themselves in the time saved in gluing, screwing and marking out.

Jacobs chuck

Usually mounted on a morse taper shaft, this makes for an extremely useful chuck, used mainly for drilling in the lathe, either rotating at the headstock end or used stationary in the tailstock. Can also be used to hold small items of turnery by gripping on a turned spigot. Mine gets used mostly for holding a calico polishing mop and small drum sander. This chuck is pretty well a must if you have no pillar drill and produce items that need drilling.

9 Other tools and accessories

The usual woodwork tools will all find a use with any turner. Saws, hammers, mallets and screwdrivers will all be necessary at some time. The turner will find he also needs several that are not in his general woodwork kit.

Calipers

Calipers of all types will be found to be indispensable. Outside calipers will prove the most useful for checking diameters and wall thicknesses, inside for checking apertures of hollow items. Double-ended, which transfer the measurement from one end to the other, are used mainly for checking for a constant wall thickness in bowls.

Dividers or compasses

Dividers or compasses in a variety of sizes are a must for marking out bowl discs and transferring measurements to rotary stock.

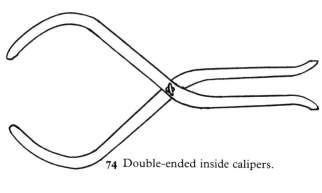

74 Double-ended inside calipers.

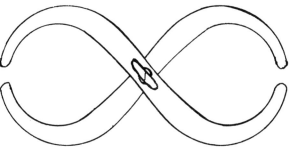

75 Double-ended outside calipers.

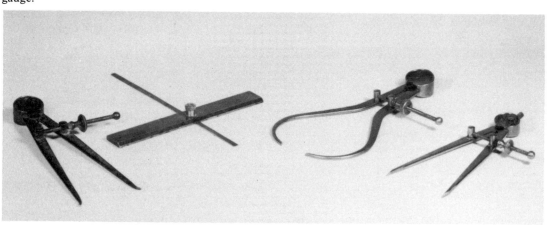

76 Selection of calipers and dividers, and depth gauge.

47

77 Setting dimension for sizing tool.

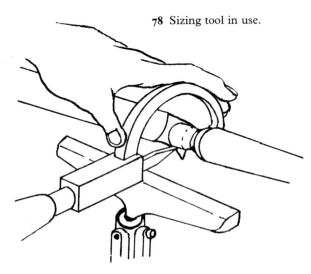

78 Sizing tool in use.

Depth gauge

A depth gauge is essential for checking depth of bowls and boxes, to make sure you do not go through the bottom.

A sizing tool

Used with a parting tool, this will enable you to produce constant diameters without the need for calipers, once set.

A steel rule

Uses obvious.

A centre finder

Allows you to find in seconds a precise centre on square, round or almost any-shaped stock.

An anglepoise lamp

Will be found to be indispensable. In my own workshop it is used as the main source of light for the lathe, and little reliance is placed on daylight, which acts as a supplement rather than a necessity.

A calico mop

For polishing bases of items like boxes or bowls. Will prove useful held in a Jacobs chuck or three-jaw.

Goggles

For use when sharpening or dealing with flawed wood on the lathe.

Face mask

For dust protection.

Suede-faced calico gloves

The type gardeners use. Will give a good grip when holding polished bowls for shaping on a drum sander or to stop hand-burn when timber spins while using a drill press.

A smock

Zipped to the neck, this will help prevent shavings getting in uncomfortable places, and minimize the trail up the stairs and in the bedroom.

A cyano-acrylic glue (such as Superglue)

Always needed in the workshop. Often used when making bowls with natural tops where splitting in the sapwood has taken place. A mixture of the dust and glue will make the edge sound.

Pencils

A turner without these is like a dog without a tail.

I could go on and on, but the above suggestions should cover most eventualities.

79 Centre finder.

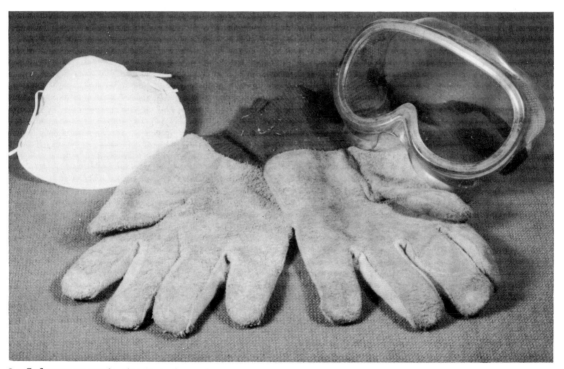

80 Safetywear: mask, gloves, and goggles.

49

10 Helpful tips on techniques

There are several areas of turning that have many similarities to driving a car or to a sport. This may seem an odd statement to make, but think about it. The grip on a steering wheel, club or bat is very important, and so is that on turning tools. Here the similarity continues, for most people, when they grip a steering wheel or golf club for the first time, hold on as though their life depended on it – often with the whites of their knuckles showing. Yes, you must grip, but in a manner that gives control to guide, not force; otherwise you will be tense, rigid, get tired quickly and have a tendency to overreact, causing jerky stunted movements where everything should be fluid and flowing for best results.

Stance, again, is vitally important. It is best if the feet are positioned in such a way that there is no need to move them throughout the cutting operations, letting the body sway gently from the ankles. To achieve this, the body weight needs to be distributed over the foot where cutting begins and transferring to the other where cutting ends. This will of course prove impossible when turning long spindles, but try and turn in as long and flowing a movement as possible. Most face-place work should prove possible to turn in this way. Figs. 81 and 82 show the sort of thing to aim for. Bowl turning has a more front-on approach, with the gouge handle often given extra support by being pulled against the body when shaping the outside, but not the inside. For spindle turning a more side-on approach is needed, as the body can get in the way at times, but again it is often used to give added support to the tool handle. Lengths of up to 380 mm (15 in) can be turned with the feet in the position shown (Fig. 83), the right foot moving to allow parting of the ends.

The form of the outside of any object is best

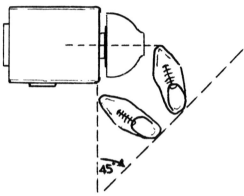

81 Foot position for turning outside of a bowl.

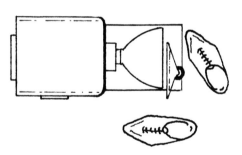

82 Foot position for turning inside of a bowl.

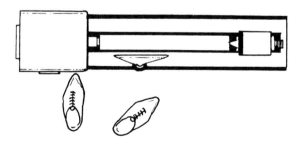

83 Foot position for general spindle turning.

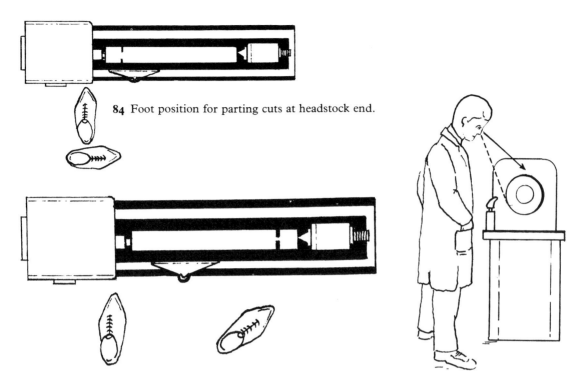

84 Foot position for parting cuts at headstock end.

85 Foot position for parting cuts at tailstock end.

86 Eye direction for profile forming.

assessed by looking across the surface when near the top of the lathe as the cutting continues, not at the area where this is happening. You can do this, but there are so many other things to take your eye: your hand, tool, rest, etc., that it is difficult to see a true profile. It is a question of looking ahead with anticipation, just as in driving or playing sport.

The majority of face-plate work should be done with a gouge, as indicated earlier. Mine all have bevels that are more obtuse than the normally recommended ones. This initially came about by mistake rather than by design, no doubt caused by lazy grinding, sharpening just the leading edge and ignoring the heel. Now it is done on purpose, for I find it allows for a much more flowing usage of the tool, particularly when hollowing out a bowl's interior. Almost any shape can be cut from the top to the centre of the base in one flowing continuous movement, with the bevel rubbing throughout. It also allows it to be used in a much more horizontal plane than can ever be achieved with a conventionally ground gouge.

Those with bedded lathes will find this of great benefit, for larger diameters can be tackled before the handle fouls on the bed.

Scrapers are something I view as a necessary evil, and restrict their use as much as possible. When used, it should be to skim ripples or unevenness from a surface, not for major shaping. Always keep them on the move, taking light passing cuts as shown in the drawings. In this way, reasonable success will be achieved.

In all turning, if you are right-handed, the left hand plays the supporting role, often with only the thumb in contact with the tool on the rest. As final shaping starts to take place, the fingers act as a steady, absorbing vibration or preventing flexing as the work becomes thinner – particularly the walls of bowls or the flange of platters. In spindle work again a steadying action is the aim, often counteracting the pressure of the cutting tools being applied in a forward movement. In all spindle work slicing cuts in the direction of the tail- or headstocks are to be recommended, for this minimizes whip and flexing on thin work.

51

87 Hand supporting a thin bowl.

88 Fingers supporting under the work of a thin spindle.

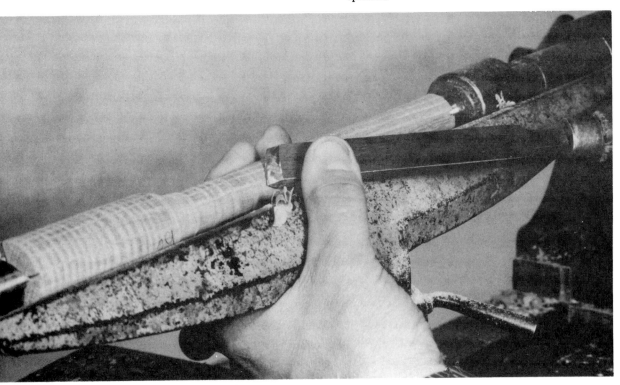

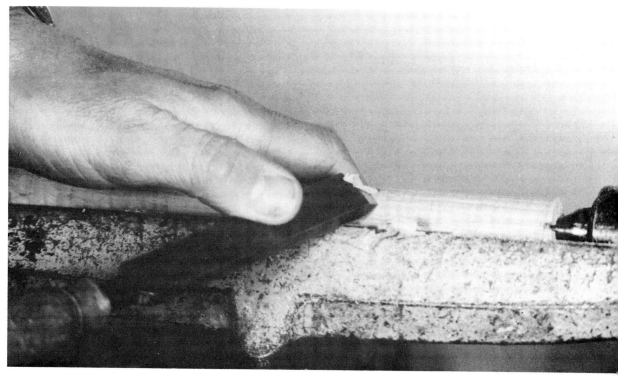

89 Fingers supporting over the work of a thin spindle.

The right hand is the one that dictates the depth, direction, and angle of cut. You will develop a strong right wrist which will enable you to make positive, controlled fluid movements that help you to reach successful conclusions.

Finally, when dealing with difficult grain areas within a piece that tears, pecks or whatever, the application of some of your finishing oils or waxes can have a magical effect, for these will soften the fibres and allow them to be cut with a great deal less trouble. Oil is the most effective, as it penetrates most easily, but its use should be avoided if you intend to use finish with a cellulose-based product, for a chemical reaction will take place, giving a white blotchy finish. If this is your intention, use paste wax instead of oil. Push wax into the torn fibres with the thumb or fingers. Penetration will be less than oil and more than one application may be needed to achieve your desired smooth surface.

These are just a few tips. Many are explained more fully in the accounts of some projects.

NB. Almost every turner develops his own technique over the years. If you have found methods you are happy with, that's fine, for there are many ways of achieving similar results. My own view is to keep an open mind on all approaches of doing things, for it is the end result you are judged by, not the way you achieve it. However, it is best if you develop techniques that allow you to work speedily, effectively, and efficiently. To this end, the methods described in this chapter and throughout the rest of the book are those I use to earn my living.

11 Finishing and finishes

This is an area that people seem to have a great deal of difficulty with. Before starting to sand any piece of work your tool work should have been completed to the best of your ability. Sanding and polishing will not correct poor tool work. It may help a little, but it will not put it right.

What abrasives should one use? For many years, garnet paper was my choice; 120 grit was the coarsest but I used mainly 150, 220, 320 grit, with occasional resort to 120 grit aluminium oxide to try to sort out some seemingly impossibly difficult grain area. Keep your tools sharp and this should not happen very often.

About 1980, I switched to silicon carbide

90 Traditional hand sanding. Note the extra pressure support of the left hand.

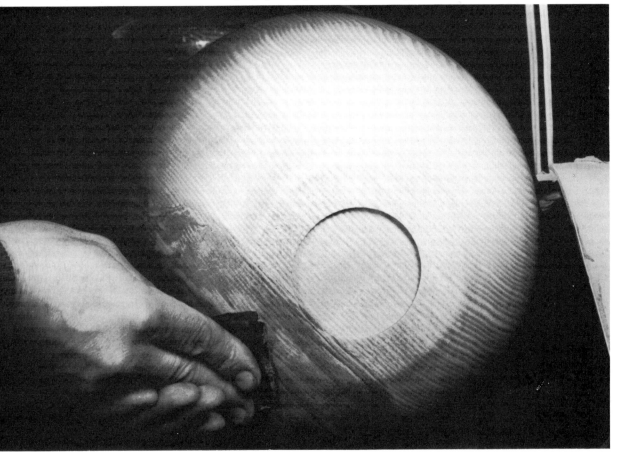

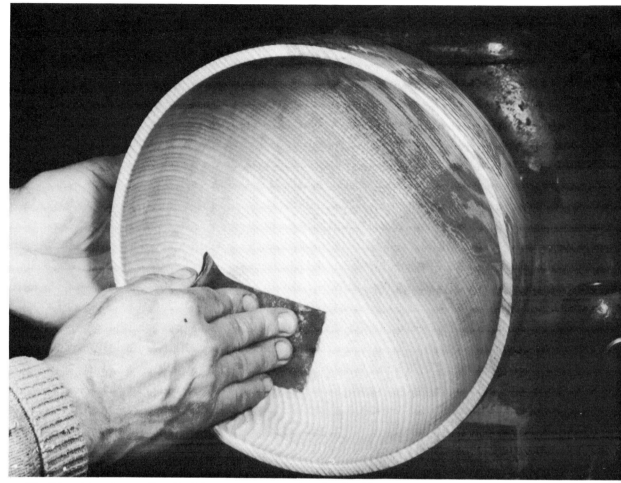

91 Traditional interior sanding. Left hand
supports the bowl's exterior to prevent flexing.

paper (wet and dry), in similar grit ratios to
garnet. This type of abrasive has various types
of backing papers. The one we turners need is
the flexi-back variety, for the normal run-of-
the-mill type, when pressure is applied, will
often allow the grit particles to part company
with their backing, clogging wood grain pores
and rendering the paper useless. The resulting
particles deposited in the grain pores will leave
the work with a dirty black look, and on light
timbers in particular this is disastrous. You will
find this does not happen with the flexi-backed
type, which, although more expensive than
garnet paper, will give a superior finish; the
abrasive lasts much longer and so cancels out
the extra cost. Another of the benefits is that

abrasive backing paper absorbs moisture from
the atmosphere, rendering garnet less effective
until it is completely dry again. Silicon carbide
(wet and dry), as the name implies, will work
equally well used wet or dry. This benefit will
become even more apparent when used with oil
finishing.

You will note that the abrasive grits I
recommend are quite fine even when first
starting to sand. This is because I feel you
should learn to turn cleanly with your tools,
and not rely on abrasives to bludgeon a finish
or shape.

Another problem with coarse abrasives is
that one particle of grit on a paper may
sometimes be harder or higher than the rest,
resulting in a deep ring scratch in your work
that will prove very difficult to remove.

The methods outlined above are those used
by most turners when sanding their work. If

55

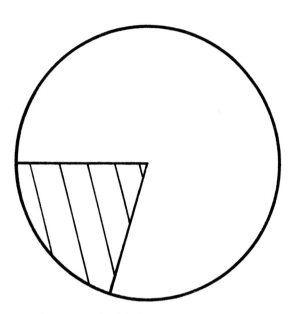

92 Area to sand safely in.

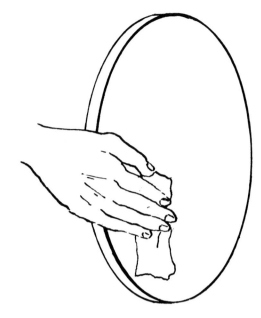

93 Fingers pointing down when sanding.

you turn thin-walled objects from exotic timbers it is possible to have surface heat cracks appear in the item, for a great deal of friction heat can be generated when a rotating surface meets a static one, such as a hand-held abrasive. This problem led to the introduction and development of the system that I now use for all my face-plate work, wherever possible: namely, foam-backed disc pads mounted in an electric drill, with lathe and drill rotating in different directions. This cuts friction heat to a minimum, making it impossible to inflict ring scratches on the work; if scratches are produced they take the form of scroll scratches which often blend with the grain of the wood.

This development came about from spending some time in David Ellsworth's workshop in the States in 1981. He used this method entirely in his finishing, using Trimite paper discs with grits from 150 down to 700; being self-adhesive they were mounted on foam-backed pads. They were all obtained from automobile repair finishing workshops, on rolls, and can also be obtained in Britain. They were, however, much too large in diameter for many of the uses I had in mind.

It is worth noting that there is nothing new in this method. Many turners in the States have been using it for years. In this country, it was mentioned to me in the early seventies as a

possibility. At that time, being somewhat conservative, I thought it sounded like cheating and did not pursue the matter. But having seen David's results, I felt it was time to try to locate something in this country. The first sort I found were in the High Street chain- and do-it-yourself stores, 127 mm (5 in) diameter rubber-backed pads with adhesive Trimite paper discs, but nothing finer than 150 grit. A continuing search unearthed abrasive discs from a pattern-makers' supplier in 25 mm (1 in); 50 mm (2 in) and 76 mm (3 in) diameters with 25 mm (1 in) foam backing on a rubber disc. This seemed to be the answer, but grits only went down to 240, so hand sanding was still needed for a finer finish. There were problems with this type as the adhesive on the disc backing seemed to be of variable quality, resulting in some discs adhering for a very short time, while others worked well. There are now many turners throughout the country using this technique, for after Nick Davidson saw the possibilities, he introduced it to his supply range of products. The problem of adhesion was noted and now we have the system of Velcro (touch-and-close fastener) on the foam pad, with fabric on the disc; the most effective method yet devised. With a much wider range of grit available, from 60 grit down to 400, this now allows complete finishing

56

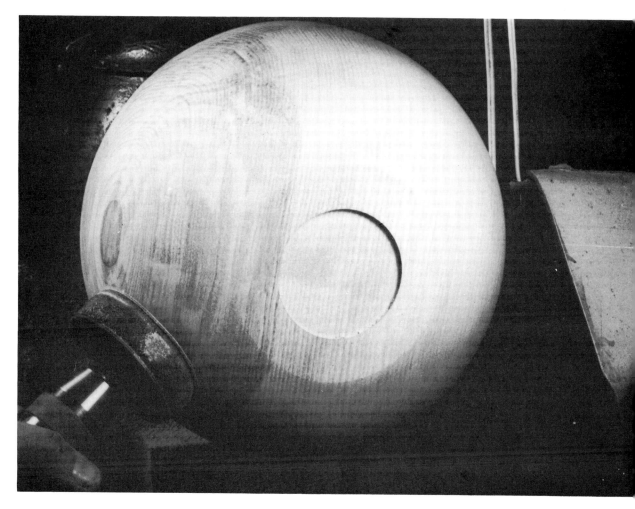

94 Power-sanding the outside of a large bowl, with the Velcro (touch-and-close fastener) system.

without having to resort to the traditional hand method. The 50 mm (2 in) and 76 mm (3 in) range will be found to have the most uses.

The results achieved by this method will be dictated by the skill of the operator, as with everything else that happens on the lathe. You will need to develop a touch and sensitivity, just as you do with your turning tools.

Depending on the diameters of the work, lathe speeds of 700–1400 r.p.m. are best; the larger the diameter, the slower the speed. Drill speeds will be best between 2,000 and 3,000 r.p.m. It is important that lathe speed shouldn't overpower the drill. For small work, up to 10 in diameter, a 400 watt drill will normally prove adequate; for larger work a 600 watt rating or higher is best, as it puts too much strain on smaller drills.

The method applied in use, if the lathe is running anti-clockwise, is to sand lightly from the centre outwards between an area of nine o'clock and seven o'clock on an imaginary clock face, or put another way, in the bottom half of the lathe's downward thrust. Do not use the full face of the rotating disc. Practice will soon dictate the way in which you use this method. Be careful not to let the drill cable touch the work or let the drill body foul the opposite edge of the work you are sanding. It's really a matter of common sense. I find that having several discs of different grits lined up is the best approach with a keyless chuck. This saves time, and the discs last longer, not being constantly peeled on and off. At the end of sanding with the finest grit, hand-held 0000 wire wool is

95 Power-sanding the interior of the bowl from Fig. 94 with the same system.

used to remove the last fine scratches. The object is now ready to accept your chosen finish. The benefits of using this method are a great saving in sanding time and a much superior finish. One drawback is dust, which is greater, due to the two rotating surfaces; hence my feelings about having good dust extraction.

Oil finishes

These are the easiest and quickest to apply and are used mainly with objects that are going to be utilitarian domestic items. The oil used is a matter of personal preference. My choice is a heavy-bodied teak oil for dark timbers and a clear teak mineral oil for light ones such as sycamore. Cooking oil, Danish oil, Tung oil are all possibilities. The latter, with several coat applications, will build up a high finish if required, but it is an expensive oil.

After you have sanded your work to your own satisfaction, apply a liberal coat of your chosen oil (with the lathe motionless) on a soft cloth. Restart the lathe, take a well-worn piece of 320 or finer (wet and dry) paper and sand the oil into the wood. This will give the work an even better finish. Stop the lathe, give the work another oil application, restart and friction dry with a dry piece of clean soft cloth. If you wish to go a stage further, take a handful of soft shavings of the same timber or something softer and give a final burnish. You will now have an object that is water-resistant for domestic use; the occasional wipe over with salad oil or cooking oil will ensure that it is kept in good order.

Shellac sealer finish

This type of finish is useful both for domestic and decorative items. After sanding, using a mop brush, apply a sparing coat of shellac-based sanding sealer, and allow to dry; the absolute minimum is fifteen minutes, but I prefer to leave it overnight. With a well-worn piece of silicon carbide (wet and dry) paper dipped in oil or wax, and with the lathe running, start to remove the excess sealer. The choice of either oil or wax will be based upon your intended final finish. The idea of dipping the mild abrasive in oil or wax is that it acts as a lubricant, stopping the build-up of excess sealer forming rings on your work, which is a common complaint if you sand dry. Next take a piece of 0000 wire wool, dip in oil or wax as with the abrasive and remove the last of the remaining excess sealer. You should now have a very smooth finish.

The use of the sealer is intended to fill the open grain pores of the timber. Left untreated, these would soon attract dust when put on display, giving the item a dingy look in a very short time. You can apply oil or wax over the finish, according to taste. If oil is selected, wipe on a coat with a soft cloth and burnish as previously described. If you decide on wax, my choice would be a 50/50 mixture of beeswax and carnauba with a little turpentine added, applied in block form. With the lathe's rotating friction, melt a thin film of wax over the work and buff with a soft cloth. The polished surface will be of a fairly high gloss. My normal method is to cut this back slightly with 0000 wire wool, giving a satin-finish look. Beeswax applied on its own is too soft and its polish is soon lost. Carnauba is too hard and brittle applied on its own, resulting in a white glass-like finish, but the mixture of the two gives the desired result.

Cellulose melamines

This is the finish I use for most items which are going to be purely decorative or are made from exotic and dense timbers. After sanding, apply a thin film of melamine with a mop brush or a cloth with the lathe stopped. Work quickly, as it dries in seconds. Try not to cause a double build-up by going over the same area twice during this application. With 0000 wire wool dipped in soft paste wax, remove and flatten surplus melamine with the lathe rotating. The wax used is of a petroleum variety that gives excellent results in conjunction with the melamine. With a little of the wax on a soft cloth, start the lathe and impart the final finish. If the gloss is too high, cut back lightly with 0000 wire wool to obtain a satin look. Melamine is water-resistant and this is the reason I use it. Decorative bowls made from dark woods such as ebony being handled in galleries by people with clammy hands, led to my use of this finish. Previously I used the shellac method, but since it was not waterproof a white fingerprint bloom was caused when it was handled. The use of melamine has solved this. You can apply more than one coat of melamine. This will build up an even more water-resistant surface but, in my view, doesn't look as natural.

One word of caution. Do not apply a petroleum-based wax over a shellac sealer. The two do not mix.

You will note there has been no mention of instant-shine polishes, polyurethane, etc. This is because of my dislike for any finish that gives a high gloss or skin-like barrier over the wood's surface. High gloss makes wood look cheap and plastic-like, while heavy build-up polishes seem to block the natural beauty of the wood. The finishes described are used for my own work and have served me well, with no complaint from customers.

12 Timber buying and problems

Buying timber is a problem we all face, professional or amateur. One of the questions I am most often asked is, 'Where do you get your timber?' The answer I give is often, 'From many sources', which is true. Most people interpret my answer as a reluctance to tell, but that is not the case. The fact is, most of my supplies come from timber yards where they don't want to know the man looking for a couple of blocks to make the odd salad bowl. You must remember that these people are used to dealing in thousands of cubic feet of timber. Many don't much like the one-man professional.

Things have changed, unfortunately, from the days when there were country sawmills all over the place and most were happy to sell you the odd block or board. If you still have one nearby, you are lucky, for most will have something that will interest you and it will normally be at a modest price. If you are not so fortunate, where do you buy? The monthly woodworking magazines are a good starting place. There are many small yards and makers who advertise timber supply. Most invite personal inspection; and that is really the only way to buy timber. There are now also many suppliers of the other needs of the turner who are stocking good supplies of timber. The advantage for the home craftsman of dealing with these people is that blocks, discs, etc. are often ready-cut for a specific purpose. You are not buying something that includes a lot of waste material; on the other hand, you will be paying for this service. All the same, this is perhaps the best way to start, for buying timber is an art in itself. You have to develop an eye, nose and instinct by experience. Even when you have gained these, luck still plays a part. This is an area that is difficult to teach anyone about. There are obvious guidelines, of course,

as with anything, but a tree is a living thing and every one is different. Of course, certain varieties have their own characteristics, but every once in a while one will come along that knocks all the known rules on the head. This is part of the fascination of wood. Many books have appeared on this subject and many more remain to be written. Guidelines can be given, but at the end of the day your own instinct, backed by a certain amount of knowledge, is the deciding factor. Even the most knowledgeable person on this subject is forever going to be surprised by some trick nature has played.

Other possible sources of timber supply for the amateur and professional alike are local tree surgeons, neighbours, landscape gardeners, building-site developers or council park departments. If you see these people felling trees it is worth asking what is going to happen to them. Often, if they are small, they will be cut up for logs or burnt on site. So for a modest price some useful timber can be obtained. (This is where the chain saw becomes a useful tool to have around.) Once you have obtained timber in this way, the next question is how you handle and treat it.

If you like wet turning then it is fairly easy; more on this later. If you wish to work with dry wood then you must convert it, bearing in mind the type of work you wish to make. Small fruit-wood logs left in the round will normally crack radially, leaving you with little useful timber. Let us look at ways of dealing with, say, a 200 mm (8 in) diameter cherry log. This is best left in its greatest possible length before the branches start to fork. Seal the ends of the log with end seal or some oil-based paint; anything to slow down the drying process, minimizing end-splitting. Now consider the type of item you hope to make from your newly acquired

96 Small radially cracked cherry log.

timber, remembering that you need to box out the centre pith core of the log and remove most of the sap wood. You will be lucky to obtain any larger pieces of timber than 125 mm × 64 mm (5 in × 2½ in), plus its length. After distortion and shrinkage you may get some small bowls, 120 mm diameter × 60 mm deep (4¾ in × 2⅜ in), from your plank. If squares are more to your liking you should get four, 64 mm × 64 mm (2½ in × 2½ in), quite comfortably from your 200 mm (8 in) log or, say, two planks 125 mm × 64 mm (5 in × 2½ in), or a combination of both: one 125 mm × 64 mm (5 in × 2½ in) plank and two squares, 64 mm × 64 mm (2½ in × 2½ in). Seasoning time will to some extent depend on storage. The

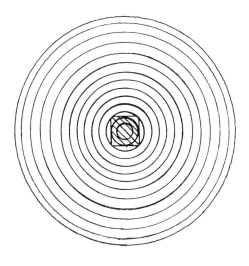

97 Log with pith core boxed out.

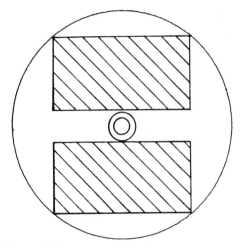

98 Log divided for small planks.

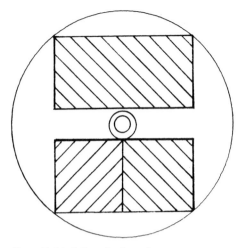

100 Log divided for plank and squares.

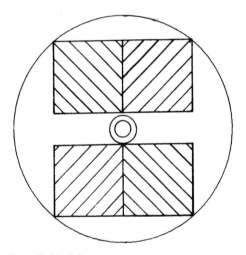

99 Log divided for squares.

'year to the inch' adage can be disregarded by and large, with these sort of sizes. Do not try and dry too quickly, for the outer edges will harden before the moisture in the centre has had a chance to escape. The best results with these sort of sizes will be obtained if the timber is kept under cover with no direct sunlight or howling wind passing through. A barn or garage with a gentle air movement can be ideal. The 64 mm × 64 mm (2½ in × 2½ in) squares have a good chance of being usable in six to nine months and the 125 mm × 64 mm (5 in × 2½ in) in eighteen months. It is better to err on the side of caution, though. Remember

that air-dried timber is unlikely to have less than a 16 per cent to 20 per cent moisture content. Most homes have central heating, with a moisture content of around 10 per cent, so all timbers should be in the warmer workshop prior to use for a month or two in these sizes, or longer for larger.

There are ways of quickening the process if you cut and turn your squares into cylinders. If condiments are something you intend to make, the hole can be drilled. All this will reduce your waiting time to weeks rather than months. However, you will find your cylinders will go oval and shrink and you will need to redrill them for the hole to be true. Rough-turning bowls while wet has been going on for centuries, then remounting for final shaping and finishing; again, ovalling will take place, reducing the finished size of the items. From a living tree to a finished bowl is easily possible within three months with this method. The drawback of the technique is the shrinkage, for the bowl you thought originally was going to be 120 mm × 60 mm (4¾ in × 2⅜ in) actually turns out something like 110 mm × 55 mm (4 in × 2 in), and squares of 64 mm × 64 mm (2½ in × 2½ in) end up as cylinders of no more than 55 mm (2 in) diameter.

There are ways of stopping this shrinkage, and one is with the use of PEG (Poly Ethylene Glycol). The wood is immersed in the solution and the natural sap and water content of the wood is replaced with the PEG. This process is called osmosis. I am not a lover of it, for it

62

101 Selection of wet rough-turned ash salad bowls.

changes the nature of the wood, making it somewhat greasy and soapy, and darkens many timbers. It also takes time and costs money, all things against it for me. It does have very useful applications, though, such as the preservation of the wooden objects taken from the *Mary Rose,* or its use in woodturning by Ed Moulthrop, allowing work to be made that would have been impossible without his personal development and use of this product. Another possibility to consider when converting your small log is to divide it up like a cake into quarters (or thirds, if decorative bowls are your forte), using the natural top including the sapwood and, if you are lucky, the bark, but still boxing out the pith core.

A point to bear in mind when buying timber is that if you are interested in something with a wild or unusual figure, it may be possible to buy for less than the mild, straight-grained varieties the timber yards normally deal in. This is mainly because most people in industry using timber don't want the trouble of it, unless, of course, the unusual figure is throughout the log, which will make it of great interest to veneer dealers, and send the price sky-high.

Selecting timbers for a specific purpose is worth a comment. Most English timber is sold with the bark on both edges of the plank, as most logs are cut through and through, or with one edge squared. It is not common to see English timbers converted into squares, etc., unless it is for fencing or gateposts, or specially requested by a customer.

Many merchants will try and sell you the top board from the stack but if you know the specific use for which you want the timber, you may require a board from lower in the stack. Insist on getting it. Some merchants may not like this, but you are spending the money.

Imagine you intend to buy a 50 mm (2 in) board which you wish to make into condiments, sugar bowls, salt bowls or shallow fruit bowls. Try to buy something that gives minimum waste. Condiments and salt bowls come from 50 mm (2 in); sugar bowls need to be 100 mm (4 in) diameter; and the fruit bowl, say, 300 mm (12 in) diameter. Try, then, to buy a board that will allow you to produce all of these items with the minimum of waste. I suggest something around 350 mm (14 in) in width. You will find it prudent to allow a sapwood waste allowance with English

63

102 660 mm (26 in) dia. tulipwood bowl by Ed Moulthrop. This would have been impossible without the use of PEG. Being end-grained, it would have cracked radially throughout.

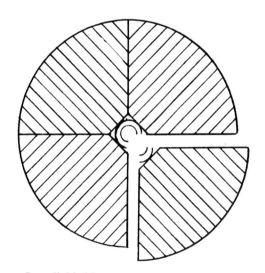

103 Log divided into quarters.

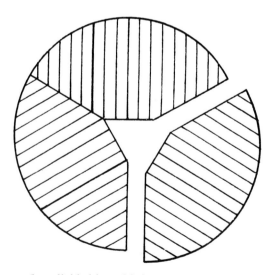

104 Log divided into thirds.

105 A fine-looking burr maple tree.

106 Typical English board with sap and bark on top. Typical imported one on the bottom, square-edged and sap-free.

107 Looks good: African blackwood on top, Brazilian tulipwood on the bottom.

timbers. In most cases it tends to be less hard than the heartwood, making it more susceptible to atmospheric changes, which may result in distortion. No hard-and-fast rules can be given on how much waste to allow. This will vary from species to species and tree to tree, even of the same species.

When buying imported timber you seldom have to make the above allowances. In most cases the sapwood has been removed at source, most being supplied as square-edged timber, often in a wide variety of sizes, making it possible to buy the exact sizes you want. If you require narrow widths, try to obtain them rather than buying a wide board and cutting them out, for this will certainly prove more expensive. Most imported timber is more expensive than the domestically grown, but there will be little or no waste.

Exotics are another world and price altogether, and it is best to wait until you have acquired a good knowledge of domestic and common imported varieties before branching out into this area. There are many more pitfalls

108 The woods from Fig. 107 turned over, showing the typical pitfalls of buying exotics.

and traps to fall into when dealing with exotics, and mistakes can prove very costly. It will be best if you have acquired a skill and flexibility within your approach to design. Often when dealing with exotics a change of direction from the originally conceived idea will prove necessary, as some unforeseen fault or blemish may appear as if from nowhere.

This brief outline on timber purchasing and its problems is designed to try to shed a little light on a vast subject in which most of us skim only the surface. Experience in dealing with it on a day-to-day basis is the only way to learn. Each timber has some peculiarity of its own, be it smell, texture, dust, a tendency to split, warp, or shrink – and this unpredictability is part of the fascination, coupled with a beauty, warmth and charm that leaves you for ever wanting to learn more of its secrets.

13 Domestic wares

This is the area in which most people with a lathe seem to work, whether they are amateur or professional. Let us consider first the type of work we are talking about: wooden kitchen utensils, dining table accessories or general useful items for anywhere around the home. In all cases, the work should be so designed that it will be fit for its intended purpose.

Kitchen wares

These items have been made for centuries and most of them fulfil the needs of their users admirably. This can be put down to their development through the years, most items being based on a well-proven formula. That is fine. Change for its own sake is worthless if a new style does not do the job as well as the old.

Many such utensils can be mass-produced, and really need to be at the lower-price end of the market, making it imperative that large quantities should be produced. For an individual trying to compete in this area it must be an occupation of soul-destroying repetitiveness. Naturally, for the home turner who is asked to make the odd item for the kitchen it is a different matter.

If you are asked to make kitchen items, timber choice is important, the proven ones in this area being sycamore, hornbeam, beech and box. These tend to be fairly bland in appearance, being close-grained, and since they are almost odourless, will not impart any taint or smell to the food. Items of this nature are best left unpolished after sanding as they are washed and scrubbed clean after use; this raises the grain slightly and is one of the reasons for selecting close-grained woods. I was once told of an old fellow who made porridge spurtles and after sanding would wet them again and again, sanding after each

application of water until it became impossible to raise the grain. The effect was to produce an almost case-hardened surface, something similar to that on the handle of a fork or spade, caused by spitting on the palm of your hand when using them.

Tableware

This is an area which affords an opportunity to produce a multitude of items that can give pleasure in use, if designed and made correctly. It is possible to have an item that looks fine but is useless for its intended purpose; by the same token it is also possible to have an item that looks dreadful but performs the function for which it was intended. Neither is altogether successful.

It should be possible for the maker to produce an item that is both pleasing to the eye and capable of fulfilling its intended function. This should be your aim when considering the intended use of the item. There are many potters and turners regretting their mistakes through losing sight of these objectives. When our economic troubles arrived people started to remember the potter's jug that looked good but did not pour well, or the woodturner's sugar bowl that tipped over when full. Unfortunately, many of the public were unable to tell the good from the bad and tarred both with the same brush. This has, however, had some good effects, for makers of inferior products have fallen by the wayside. Those that have remained have taken note and are now producing better wares.

If you take a close look at most wooden tableware you will notice a certain blandness about it. Why is this so? There are several answers. One is that the makers select timber that works well, is mild-grained and gives the least trouble. Another is that they are concerned only with certain basic shapes which allow an item to fulfil its intended function. Thirdly, and perhaps most importantly, price. It is the combination of these factors that results in an impression of blandness.

Looking at these factors one at a time, there are reasons for each. Price is certainly a factor with domestic ware, for the general public seems to have a preconceived idea of the range of prices they are prepared to pay for certain items. The maker who produces work at the upper end of this mentally set price range should be able to produce good-quality work of acceptable design and function and earn a reasonable living for himself. Those who produce at the lower end of the price scale will normally make items that fall down on both counts. Shops stocking both types of work normally find that the quality product sells before the inferior one despite its higher price. Those shops stocking just one grade of work often find a market, too, for the shop stocking quality attracts the customer looking for quality. Those stocking inferior styles also have their patrons. I suppose one way or another the public gets what it wants, or deserves.

From the maker's viewpoint, though, I am at a loss to know why he or she should want to produce work of poor quality. The time difference in making something well or badly is small, but the difference in the end product is great. A poor-quality craftsman is also doing himself, the public and the craft a disservice. One of the points of making by hand is surely to produce something worthwhile and better than can be made by machine, and getting satisfaction from doing so. Poor-quality handwork is worthless, and a machine may do it better.

The choice of timber is an important factor when producing tableware. A regular supply of similar varieties is needed if you intend to sell to shops on a regular basis. Customers may purchase your complete range over a period of time and try to match things up. A common theme should be developed within your designs so that a style of your own becomes apparent to the customer. In your range of smaller items you will find it possible to offer several timbers such as walnut, yew, cherry, sycamore, ash and elm. All these will work well, but only ash, elm and sycamore should be offered in your larger range, for the others will prove difficult to obtain in any real size.

14 Designs for the home

The aim of designing and making useful products for around the home should be to make them a pleasure both to use and to look at. If you are able to achieve these two objectives you are a long way towards making something worth while.

Two items for the kitchen

I shall describe a chopping board and mortar and pestle, both of these items somewhat heavier and chunkier than any of the others suggested for around the home. This is due to the fact that you expect them to be in almost daily use and subjected to more knocks and hard usage than many of the other items. Their intended uses almost decree that they be made in such a way.

Chopping board
A disc of 38 mm (1½ in) sycamore, quarter-sawn if possible to minimize any chance of distortion, is ideal. If this is not possible, use something that is well seasoned and has not been fast grown. This you can judge by the spacing of the growth rings; the more widely spaced, the softer and faster-grown the timber, making it more susceptible to the absorption of moisture, something that is usually present in a kitchen. This will almost certainly lead to distortion, making the board rock in use: something to be avoided when using sharp knives. So try and select a close-grained timber. This will absorb less atmospheric moisture and will stand up to the constant knife cuts with less surface degrade when in constant use. The choice of size is a matter of personal preference, but 230 mm (9 in) diameter is about the smallest useful size, and 405 mm (16 in) diameter approx. is perhaps the maximum. Any size within these suggestions you will be

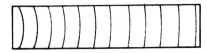

109 Fast-grown quarter-sawn section.

110 Fast-grown through-sawn section.

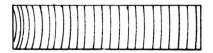

111 Slow-grown quarter-sawn preferred.

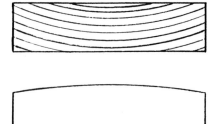

112 Slow-grown through-sawn, best used in this manner.

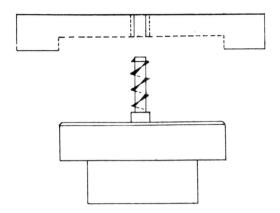

113 Screw chuck with wooden disc.

114 Trueing the face with 12 mm ($\frac{1}{2}$ in) high-speed steel bowl gouge.

able to turn on a screw chuck if of the parallel-machined variety. Up to 300 mm (12 in) diameter will mount successfully on a screw chuck of 100 mm (4 in) diameter. Over this size a wooden back plate to increase the load bearing will prove beneficial. My reason for suggesting a screw chuck is that this will leave you with only one hole to fill in the base, rather than two or three if you use a face plate. Other mounting methods could be used, e.g. glue, joints, etc., but these are mostly slow, wasteful and messy.

You will need to prepare the base prior to mounting in the lathe, as you are not going to be able to turn it unless you friction-grip the disc in some way to allow you to do so. If you have a planer or large sander then there is no problem. Failing this, hand-plane the base true and flat across the grain and sand to finish.

115 The edges being shaped with 12 mm ($\frac{1}{2}$ in) spindle gouge with bowl gouge angles.

Drill a pilot hole in the centre of the base 6 mm ($\frac{1}{4}$ in) diameter and some 16 mm ($\frac{5}{8}$ in) deep. Mount the disc on the screw chuck. Lathe speed is best around the 800 r.p.m. area for all of the suggested sizes. Make sure the disc is clear of the tool rest and true up the outside diameter with a sharp 12 mm ($\frac{1}{2}$ in) high-speed steel bowl gouge. Having done this, move the rest into position for truing-up the face. It is best set parallel to the face, slightly below centre. With the same gouge, start to true the face, working from the middle to outside edge. With the index finger under the gouge resting on the tool rest and with the thumb on top, pull the gouge towards you. This will give you a traversing effect that should result in your achieving a very true face from the gouge with few undulations. Practice and mastery of this method will prove to be of great benefit when making any item that demands a true flat surface.

You should now have a true edge and face from the gouge, but with hard square corners that are not pleasing to the eye or for use. Move the tool rest back to the edge and with a 12 mm ($\frac{1}{2}$ in) spindle-gouge, fingernail-shaped, but with a bowl-gouge ground angle, pull the gouge towards you from both the top and the bottom face towards the centre of the edge, creating a soft radius. The required shape has now been created, but will benefit from the use of a 31 mm ($1\frac{1}{4}$ in) high-speed steel square-ended scraper just to remove any slight surface ripples created by the gouges. Again, set the tool rest parallel with the face, but in this case

Brazilian tulipwood box, 75 mm (3 in) high x 60 mm (2⅜ in) dia.

Below Boxes, left to right: olivewood, putumuju, birdseye maple. Largest 70 mm (2¾ in) high x 50 mm (2 in) dia.

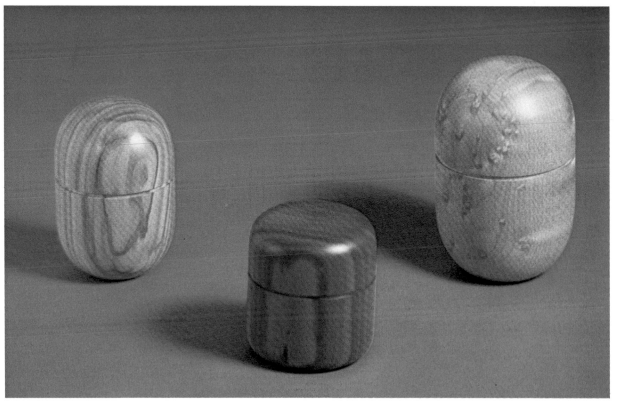

Burr elm bowl, 285 mm (11⅛ in) dia. x 100 mm (4 in) high.

Californian-grown English walnut dish, 230 mm (9¹/₁₆ in) dia. x 50 mm (2 in) high.

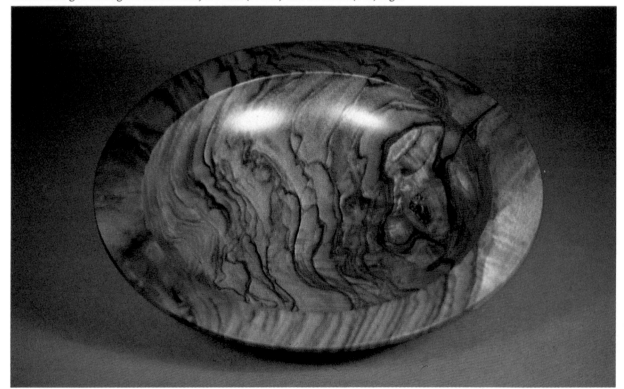

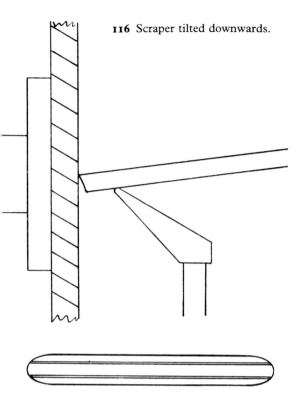

116 Scraper tilted downwards.

117 Finished chopping board.

at centre height or slightly above, for scrapers tilt downwards to cut on their top edge burr. The index finger under the scraper in contact with the tool rest, just as with the gouge, will allow you to traverse a true surface. Blend the radius on the edge both top and bottom with the scraper, and the chopping board is now finished and ready for sanding. Perhaps a couple of little vee grooves on the edge will give an extra touch that can be incorporated in all the domestic projects throughout, giving a simple linked theme. This is best done with a small diamond-point scraper.

Power-sand with a 75 mm (3 in) Velcro disc, with 180, 240, 400 grit abrasives, or your own method, and your board is almost complete. A liberal coat of clear teak mineral oil sanded in with a well-worn 320 wet and dry, plus a further coat of oil burnished with its own shavings, should provide you with a well-made functional chopping board. Remove the board from the screw chuck and fill the screw hole with plastic wood or wooden plug. Let filler or glue dry, sand and finish.

Mortar and pestle
The materials needed for this proposed design are a disc 125 mm (5 in) × 75 mm (3 in) for the mortar, and 150 mm (6 in) long, 38 mm (1½ in) square for the pestle. The mortar bowl requirements are very different from almost any other sort of bowl, namely, it will be used to have herbs and spices pounded up in it, so the design calls for it to be somewhat heavier in section than most other bowls. As with anything that is going to contain powder or small granules, it is best if the inside of the bowl is incurved or at least straight, certainly not openly dished or flared. The design shown in Fig. 120 fulfils all these requirements and is intended to be held comfortably in the hand against the body, giving support while pounding with the pestle. In addition, when put on the kitchen shelf it has a pleasing profile.

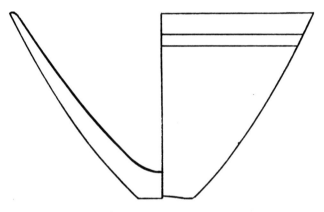

118 Open bowl, weak in form for its purpose.

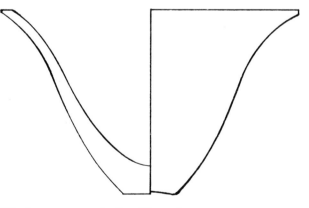

119 A worse example than Fig. 118.

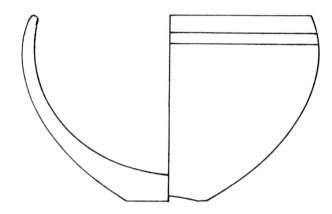

120 A proven design.

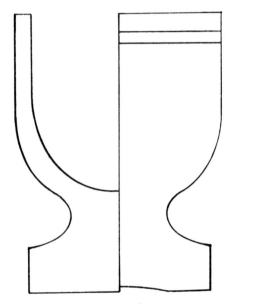

121 Another design which works.

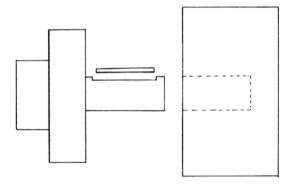

122 Pin chuck with prepared bowl blank.

The methods of making and chucking depend on personal preference. The ones described here are those I prefer.

Drill a 25 mm (1 in) hole with a forstner or saw-tooth bit in the centre of your bowl disc, stopping 18 mm ($\frac{3}{4}$ in) short of the base. Mount your disc on a 25 mm (1 in) diameter pin chuck. This is a quick and easy holding method, giving you the advantage when hollowing out the inside of an automatic depth stop from your drill hole, and making it easier to open up, as there is a hole down the middle. This is true when hollowing out any bowl as it allows you to work from the top to the base in one sweeping movement. Lathe speed should be around 1,300 r.p.m. Shape the exterior of the bowl with the 12 mm ($\frac{1}{2}$ in) high-speed steel bowl gouge, removing wood from the base towards the top in easy fluid movements. Maximum diameter is best about 15 mm ($\frac{5}{8}$ in) from the top. The actual diameter of the outside top edge is best 6 mm ($\frac{1}{4}$ in); 8 mm ($\frac{5}{16}$ in) smaller than the maximum. The diameter of the base should be around 38 mm ($1\frac{1}{2}$ in) to 41 mm ($1\frac{5}{8}$ in). The curves, within these constraints, will fall easily into place. Final shaping is with the 31 mm ($1\frac{1}{4}$ in) square-ended scraper. Two little vee grooves near the top with the diamond-point scraper will keep going the theme mentioned earlier.

The turning of the inside will be on the screw chuck, so the base should be made slightly concave and a pilot hole drilled in the base. This is done by way of a 6 mm ($\frac{1}{4}$ in) drill some 12 mm ($\frac{1}{2}$ in) deep, hand-held in a tool handle and pushed right into the middle of the base to give an accurate remounting hole. A piece of tape or depth stop will stop you going right through the base.

Sand the outside at this stage and oil. Remove from the pin chuck and mount on the parallel-machined screw chuck. Hollowing out the inside should be achieved with the 12 mm ($\frac{1}{2}$ in) high-speed steel bowl gouge, or if you find this too large use a 6 mm ($\frac{1}{4}$ in) high-speed steel bowl gouge. It should be possible to shape the whole interior with a gouge but if you have problems use a 38 mm ($1\frac{1}{2}$ in) round-nose scraper to remove any ripples or high spots.

Sand the interior with 50 mm (2 in) Velcro (touch-and-close) sanding discs: 120, 180, 240, and 400 grits are my suggestion. Oil as described in the finishing section. Remove

123 Shaping the mortar bowl outside with a 12 mm (½ in) bowl gouge. Note thumb only is on the top of the gouge.

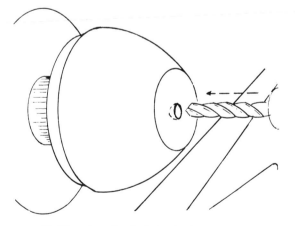

124 Drilling the pilot hole in the base.

from the screw chuck, fill or plug the screw hole and when dry, finish off.

The pestle should be mounted between centres, turned to a cylinder and roughly shaped with an 18 mm (¾ in) or 31 mm (1¼ in) high-speed steel roughing gouge. Final shaping is best done with an 18 mm (¾ in) high-speed steel skew chisel, the bulbous end towards the headstock for ease of turning. It will prove necessary to blend the shaft of the pestle at the hand-held end with a small spindle gouge. You may also find it easier to shape the small handle with a 9 mm (⅜ in) beading tool. This will also allow you to cut two vee grooves in the shaft, in keeping with those on the bowl.

Hand-sand with 150, 240, 320 grits (wet and dry), oil and friction-dry. Remove from the lathe, cut off any surplus material at each end and hand-sand or buff-sand on a foam drum sander.

125 The pestle being shaped with a 18 mm ($\frac{3}{4}$ in) high-speed steel skew chisel.

126 Pestle knob handle being shaped with a 9 mm ($\frac{3}{8}$ in) beading tool.

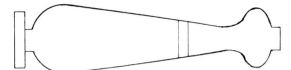

127 Waste material on the pestle.

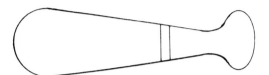

128 Pestle completed.

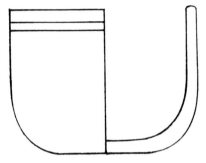

129 Ideal shape for salt or sugar.

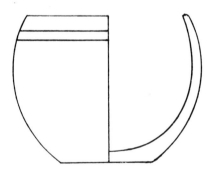

130 Another ideal shape for salt or sugar.

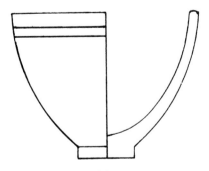

131 Easily tipped in use.

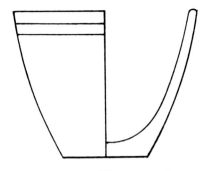

132 Too open a shape.

The chopping board and mortar bowl are the only two projects that will have screw holes in them, and are fairly basic utilitarian items, not requiring the same degree of refinement as other items for the dining table.

Items for the dining table

The first two suggestions require a similar design principle to the mortar, as they are to be used for holding small granules. They are a salt bowl and spoon and a sugar bowl and spoon. As indicated earlier, anything intended to hold small particles is best incurved or straight-sided. Also, it is important that such items should be stable in use. Once more, the intended function puts some constraint upon the design if a successful article is to be produced.

The designs in Figs 129 and 130 will fulfil these ideals admirably. Both are also pleasing to the eye, despite the fact that their base size is almost two-thirds of the maximum diameter. It would be fair to say that any bowl that is intended for table use should have a base size of no less than one-third of the bowl's maximum diameter. That is not to say that a bowl cannot have a smaller base, but for functional purposes, stability is of prime importance. Any decrease in the size of base suggested will lead to an easily tipped and generally less stable object.

Fig. 131 shows exactly this point. Although pleasing to look at, it would be likely to be tipped over in use. The bowl in Fig. 132 may prove fairly stable in use, but the shape is not suitable for its function; it is too open, making

133 Cylinder turned with spigot.

the granules easy to spill and difficult to scoop when the content is low.

Salt bowl

If making more than one of these items it will be easier to make two from one cylinder of wood. As the bowls are tiny, it is best to make them from end-grained timber. A piece 90 mm (3½ in) long by 50 mm (2 in) square will allow two bowls to be made. Mount between centres, turn to a cylinder with a roughing gouge, and square each end with a parting tool. The speed of the lathe should be around 1,300 r.p.m. At this stage you need to decide how you are going to chuck the bowls for hollowing out. My choice is to use the 38 mm (1½ in) precision-spigot type. To use this, a spigot 3 mm (⅛ in) long by 38 mm (1½ in) diameter must be created at one end of your cylinder, slightly undercut to make maximum use of the dovetail-type grip of this chuck. Remove from between centres and mount in the spigot chuck. True up the cylinder with an 18 mm

134 Cylinder in the spigot chuck marked out for parting.

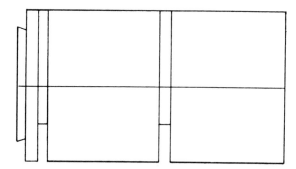

135 Cylinder marked out and parted.

($\frac{3}{4}$ in) skew chisel. This is best achieved by setting the tool rest well above centre height and parallel with the cylinder. My preference is for the point of the skew to lead, but some people may prefer the heel to do so. Whichever method you choose the tool grip is the same.

The index finger is underneath the chisel in contact with the tool rest, this being used as a guide to the chisel to obtain a traversing effect. The thumb is on top of the tool acting as a steady, applying a light even pressure to keep the tool in constant contact with the rest. Light cuts are made towards the headstock. This method should produce a smooth, true cylinder. Set a pair of dividers to 35 mm ($1\frac{3}{8}$ in) and mark the cylinder with the lathe running, then using a 3 mm ($\frac{1}{8}$ in) parting tool cut in some 12 mm ($\frac{1}{2}$ in) deep on the marked lines. This gives the overall height of the two bowls. At this stage the 18 mm ($\frac{3}{4}$ in) skew chisel, with the point leading, can be used to create the radius at the bowl base. The point can also be used to continue the two-vee-groove theme

136 Shaping the salt bowl base with the point of the skew chisel leading.

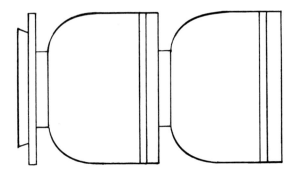

137 Finished outside profile of the bowls.

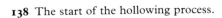

138 The start of the hollowing process.

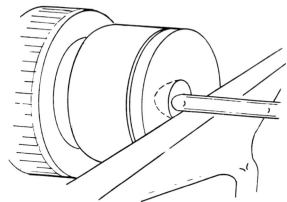

139 Hollowing the interior with a 6 mm ($\frac{1}{4}$ in) high-speed steel spindle gouge with a 60°–65° angle.

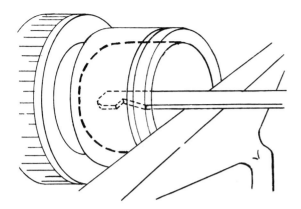

140 Final scraping of the inside.

near the top, but if you prefer, the parting tool or diamond point can be used instead. The outside of the bowls are now complete, apart from sanding. Position your tool rest across the face of your top bowl, just below centre right. Take a 6 mm ($\frac{1}{4}$ in) or 9 mm ($\frac{3}{8}$ in) standard high-speed steel spindle gouge, fingernail shaped but with a 60–65° angle; not the 30° normally associated with spindle gouges. Present the gouge to the centre of the bowl on its edge, with its open face towards you, horizontal to the bed. Tilt the face of the gouge

away from you some 10°–15° out of vertical. Now push in towards the headstock. You will find it acts just like a drill. This is the best method for hollowing any object from end grain, from egg cups to boxes. Set a depth gauge to a depth that will leave you with 3 to 4 mm ($\frac{1}{8}$ to $\frac{3}{16}$ in) of material in the base of the bowl.

Opening up the bowl is done by making a series of cuts from the centre hole that move both outwards and towards you from the base. The short bevel of the gouge will allow it still to rub during most of the hollowing process. Final shaping is with a 25 mm (1 in) round-nosed scraper, again working from the base, moved outwards and drawn up towards you. The wall thickness of the bowl should not be greater than 3 mm ($\frac{1}{8}$ in). Sanding and oiling can now take place. The only thing left to do is to part off the first bowl with the 3 mm ($\frac{1}{8}$ in) parting tool. The base can now be disc-sanded and oiled. You now have access to hollow out the second bowl, following exactly the same procedures. Please note that these methods of hollowing out only apply to objects that are made from end-grain material. Cross-grain

141 First bowl finished and parted off.

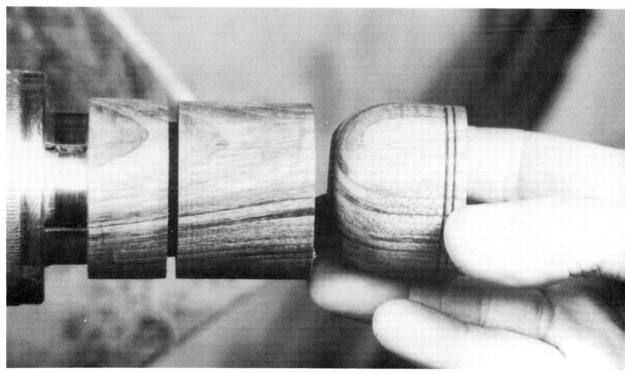

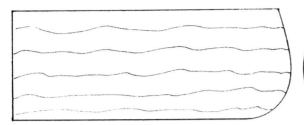

142 A cross-grained timber section.

143 An end-grained timber section.

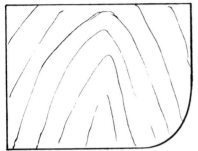

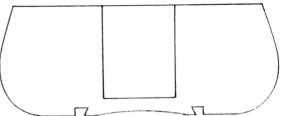

144 Profile of a finished bowl, showing the pin chuck hole and spigot remounting recess.

hollowing is always from top to bottom, not from bottom to top as described above.

Sugar bowl
The design requirements are similar to those of the salt bowl. A disc 100 mm (4 in) × 50 mm (2 in) is required, and should be cross-grained in section. The principles normally applied when deciding on the choice of grain direction are: if the diameter is greater than the height use cross grain, but if smaller, use end grain.

145 Spigot being marked out with dividers.

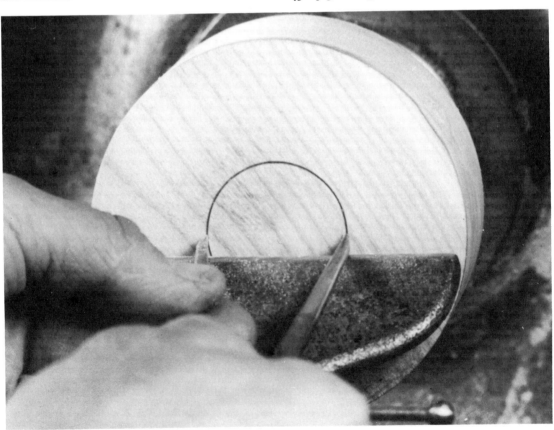

The reasons are normally strength, stability, ease of working and availability. There are some exceptions, as the salt bowl proved. Normally this is when the item is small or the turner is trying to obtain some special effect. The chucking of the sugar bowl is by way of the pin chuck for the outside and 38 mm (1½ in) spigot for the inside.

Methods of making are similar to those employed in making the mortar bowl. A 25 mm (1 in) hole drilled centrally, stopping short of the base by about 7 to 8 mm ($\frac{5}{16}$ in) will act as a depth set when hollowing out the inside. Mount on the 25 mm (1 in) pin chuck and form the outside with a 12 mm (½ in) high-speed steel bowl gouge. Complete final surface shaping with a 38–25 mm (1½–1 in) square-ended scraper.

The base should be slightly concave so that it doesn't rock, remaining stable on the table. A small spigot recess must be formed in the base at this stage. Set a pair of dividers to 38 mm

146 Outside of the completed bowl, showing the spigot recess.

(1½ in) and mark this diameter on the base. Use a 3 mm ($\frac{1}{8}$ in) parting tool to cut a recess to some 3 mm ($\frac{1}{8}$ in) maximum depth, then slightly undercut the spigot so that the dovetail action will be used to its maximum effect.

Cut two small vee grooves near the top of the bowl to continue the theme developed in the previous project. Power-sand with a 50 mm (2 in) Velcro disc with various grits or your preferred method and oil-finish.

Remove from the lathe and mount on the spigot chuck. Hollow out with a 6 mm (¼ in) high-speed steel bowl gouge, working from the top towards the base; the opposite method to that used when working with end grain. This is the best method when hollowing any cross-grained items. As the wall thickness of the bowl decreases it will be helpful for the four fingers of the left hand to cup the outside of the bowl,

147 Bowl being hollowed with a 6 mm ($\frac{1}{4}$ in) high-speed steel bowl gouge with the fingers cupping the outside.

148 Scraper in use, with the fingers again cupping the outside.

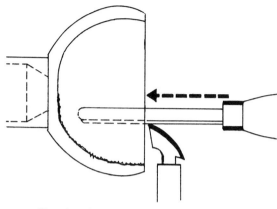

149 Showing the scraper being pushed correctly.

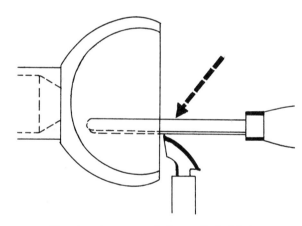

150 Showing the scraper being pulled; this is incorrect.

with just the thumb left to steady and guide the gouge. The fingers will absorb any vibration or flexing of the bowl that could cause ripples in the surface. Once the wall thickness is near 4–5 mm ($\frac{5}{32}$ in) lightly skim the surface with a selected scraper suitable for the shape of the interior. If your design is similar to that in Fig. 130 two scrapers may be needed: a square-ended one for the base and either a round-nosed or side-cutting one to blend the surfaces. You will find it best to push the scraper

towards the bottom from the top, lightly skimming any gouge marks, rather than to pull the scraper towards the side, for this can easily cause tool chatter that could even result in the cracking of a thin-walled item. Again, the fingers should cup the outside of the bowl with the thumb remaining on top of the scraper. Remember, use the scraper only if necessary, and even then, keep it to the minimum. Sand and oil in your preferred way, and your sugar bowl is complete.

Sugar and salt spoon
As these two items have the same principles and processes of making, they are described together, the only difference being in their size. As the name suggests, they are more spoon-like than scoop-like, although perhaps a more accurate definition would be spoon/scoops or scoop/spoons, for they combine the main features of these two items. A scoop normally has a short stubby handle often shorter than the bowl area, which has an open end and top. The handle of a spoon normally makes up two-thirds of its length and is only open at the top of the bowl area. The design given in Fig. 153 here combines a spoon-like handle with a scoop-like bowl.

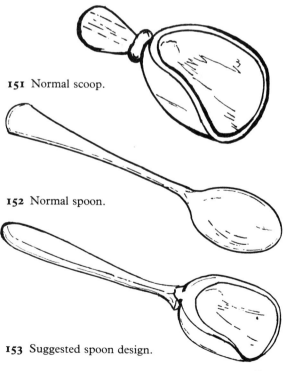

151 Normal scoop.

152 Normal spoon.

153 Suggested spoon design.

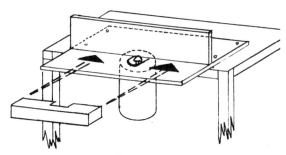

154 Spoon router jig.

The method described to make these items may not be possible if you do not possess a router, so I will suggest a few alternative methods which are often used in producing this sort of item.

Material for the sugar spoon should be straight and close-grained, 125 mm (5 in) long by 31 mm ($1\frac{1}{4}$ in) square; for the salt spoon, 75 mm (3 in) long by 12 mm ($\frac{1}{2}$ in) square. For ease of routing, 150 mm (6 in) long will be best, giving you something to grip, and you should obtain two spoons from it. Add at least 25 mm (1 in) to these suggested lengths for other methods of making, and an increase in size of the square section, say to 38 mm ($1\frac{1}{2}$ in) and 15 mm ($\frac{5}{8}$ in) respectively, will prove beneficial.

The inside of the bowl-like end is created by pushing down on top of a round-nosed cutter with the router set, as if using a spindle moulder. A wooden jig clamped or screwed to the router's fence to admit the 31 mm ($1\frac{1}{4}$ in) square for the sugar spoon, and another admitting the 12 mm ($\frac{1}{2}$ in) salt spoon, should be made. These are set in position centrally over the cutter, making it possible for an even

155 Pushing a sugar spoon square on to a router cutter.

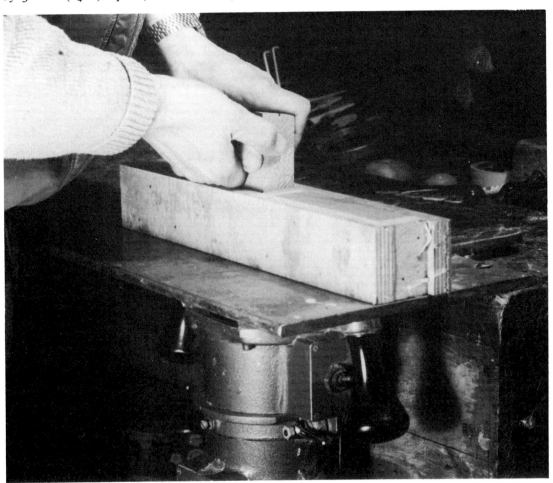

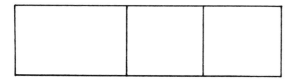

156 Spoon square marked out prior to routing.

157 Sugar spoon after routing.

158 Salt spoons after routing.

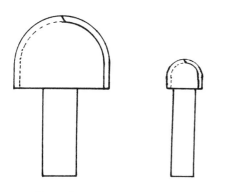

159 Domed router cutters.

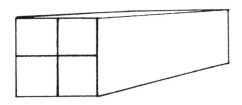

160 Block with end saw cut.

wall thickness to be produced. Push the 31 mm ($1\frac{1}{4}$ in) square into the jig hole until it rests on the top of the cutter. This is done with the router switched off. Mark a line with a pencil on your square level with your jig top. Remove and measure up 34 mm ($1\frac{3}{8}$ in) from your pencil line and square another one here. This is your stop line when you push down on the router cutter. This line can be used to mark out as many squares as you have prepared and enable you to produce a constant depth in all of them.

The aim is to produce a square with a 34 mm ($1\frac{3}{8}$ in) deep domed hole, 25 mm (1 in) in diameter, by using a 25 mm (1 in) round-nosed cutter. The reason for these considered sizes is that after all the shaping has taken place, the spoon will hold a measure of sugar similar to a normal heaped teaspoon – bringing us back to the intended purpose of the item. It will be found advantageous if a small cutter, say 18 mm ($\frac{3}{4}$ in), is used first, for this will greatly reduce the resistance that you will experience if you push straight down on to a 25 mm (1 in). It will also help the cutter keep its edge longer, give cleaner cutting and reduce the likelihood of burning the wood – something that is always possible when attempting this sort of thing. Carbide-tipped cutters are best, but high-speed steel will do. Whichever you use, keep them sharp. All this may sound a long and somewhat complicated process, but if you own a router and the necessary cutters, once you have jigged yourself up it takes seconds rather than minutes to produce your domed hole. The 31 mm ($1\frac{1}{4}$ in) square should be a good fit in your jig, for if there is much slop there will be cutter chatter, resulting in a ragged surface.

The method of producing the domed hole in the salt scoop is identical, except that the cutter needed is small: 9 mm ($\frac{3}{8}$ in) in diameter, and the hole should only be 15 mm ($\frac{5}{8}$ in) deep. This is put into either end of the 150 mm (6 in) square and then cut in half, giving you two spoons 75 mm (3 in) in length.

Saw-cut a cross on the handle end of your square to allow the spurs of a four-pronged drive centre to grip without undue pressure being required from the tailstock end. A revolving cone centre is a must for this operation. Your wall thickness at the spoon end is quite thin, and any undue pressure could split it. Reduce your square into a cylinder with either a 9 mm ($\frac{3}{8}$ in) spindle gouge or a 18 mm

161 Spoon cylinder being marked out with dividers.

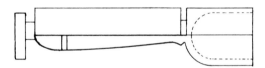

162 Top: the spoon with parted guidelines; bottom: the completed spoon's profile.

($\frac{3}{4}$ in) skew chisel. Set a pair of dividers to around 40 mm ($1\frac{9}{16}$ in) and mark a line from the tailstock end. Take a 3 mm ($\frac{1}{8}$ in) parting tool and part in on this line until something around 12 mm ($\frac{1}{2}$ in) diameter is achieved.

Reduce the handle size with the gouge. Now with the 18 mm ($\frac{3}{4}$ in) skew chisel, shape and true up the bowl and handle. It is best for the point to lead throughout. Put in the two theme vee grooves near the handle end, sand and oil-finish. Remove the waste material at the handle end, then with the sanding disc shape the spoon end, sand internally and oil-finish.

The whole process, from selecting your wood to the finished product, should take no longer than ten minutes, much less for the salt spoon. The overall finished lengths should be around 115 mm ($4\frac{1}{2}$ in) and 64 mm ($2\frac{1}{2}$ in) respectively. Alternative methods for producing these items are as follows; the first described is the most commonly used.

Mount a wooden disc on a face plate or within a cup chuck, and turn a tapered hole in the centre, creating a morse taper effect. Go right through, so a knockout bar can be used to remove waste material (a hollow spindle is, of course, necessary). The spoons have a taper turned on them between centres compatible with that in your wooden block. Tap this into the chuck with a mallet as true as you can. Hollow out the spoon bowl with gouge and scraper as described in making a salt bowl. Turning the handle and spoon bowl outside may cause difficulties without tailstock support, but normally finger support from the left hand is adequate.

If any difficulty is experienced, bring up the tailstock with its revolving centre. After turning, sanding, oiling, etc., knock out and disc-sand to shape as described above.

163 Spoon near completion being shaped with an 18 mm ($\frac{3}{4}$ in) skew chisel.

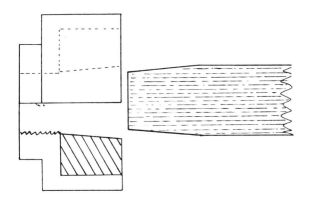

164 Cup chuck with a tapered wooden inset plus the tapered spoon blank.

165 Blank prepared for collet or Jacobs chuck.

Other possible methods of holding are by the use of collet or Jacobs chuck. In both cases, parallel diameters should be turned that will make it possible to turn spoons of the desired size. The methods of hollowing the spoon and shaping the handle are exactly as used for the tapered chuck.

Pepper mills
These are items which most households possess, but the quality of their design is variable in the extreme. Often they are copy-lathe produced from poor-quality timber. Many are stained to represent something they are not, and often the mechanism will last weeks rather than years.

If you decide to make one, buy a quality mechanism and design something that is balanced, looks good and is a pleasure to use. It is usual for this type of product to feel good in use, if it looks good. Do avoid buying those glass middle-inserts that are available, and capping them with wood at the base and top. Most are made from glass that one can only describe as being of fairground quality. In any case you will spend more time in preparing and

166 The finished articles.

fitting them up than in actually turning them –
one of my prime reasons for avoiding anything
that demands accessories. However, a pepper
mill is a very useful table item and there is no
earthly reason why it should not be possible to
make a really good one.

The most common fault one sees in the
design of these items is that they are
unbalanced; often they are too small in
diameter at the base for their height, or, if the
diameter is large enough, shape and form starts
too near the base, making the item appear
unbalanced. It's all a question of proportion.

One major principle to bear in mind is to
have no part of the design greater in diameter
than the base. This will considerably increase
your chances of success.

As to the diameter-to-height equation, a
152 mm (6 in) mill should finish not less than
54 mm (2$\frac{1}{8}$ in) in diameter, 203 mm (8 in) ×
57 mm (2$\frac{1}{4}$ in) diameter, 254 mm (10 in) ×
60 mm (2$\frac{3}{8}$ in) diameter, 304 mm (12 in) ×
64 mm (2$\frac{1}{2}$ in) diameter. These sizes are given
as guides, but anything less in terms of
diameter will make the job of creating a
balanced design more difficult, and stability on
the table will be reduced. It is worth noting
that the wooden area will normally finish 9 mm

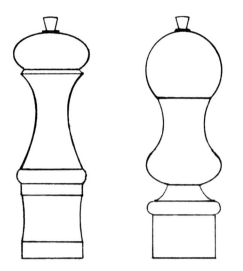

167 Poor designs, with bases too small in diameter, and displaying other features out of proportion.

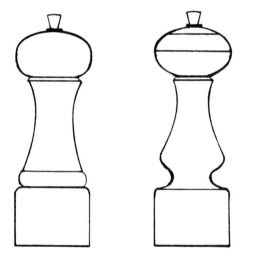

168 Designs with balanced proportions.

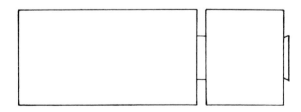

169 Cylinder with the lid parted and the spigot formed.

to 12 mm ($\frac{3}{8}$ in to $\frac{1}{2}$ in shorter than the expressed mill size, for this is inclusive of the knob.

Now to the making. Allow 12 mm ($\frac{1}{2}$ in) over the mechanism length, and 3 mm ($\frac{1}{8}$ in) or more on your desired finished diameter size, e.g. a 152 mm (6 in) mill requires timber 165 mm ($6\frac{1}{2}$ in) long and 57 mm ($2\frac{1}{4}$ in) square, allowing suitable proportional increments on other sizes. Mount the square between centres and turn to a parallel cylinder with a 31 mm ($1\frac{1}{4}$ in) roughing gouge, or your preferred tool, using a parting tool to make each end square. Now you have to make your first decision with regard to proportion of body size to knob; 108 mm ($4\frac{1}{4}$ in) body length usually gives good proportion. The prospective body will be made between centres, and the knob on the 25 mm (1 in) spigot chuck.

Cut a 25 mm (1 in) diameter spigot 3 mm ($\frac{1}{8}$ in) long at the tailstock end with a parting tool or skew chisel, measure 108 mm ($4\frac{1}{4}$ in) from the headstock end, mark with dividers or pencil, and part in.

Remove from the lathe and cut the top from the base. It is now time to drill the body. A pillar drill press is the best tool to use, with forstner or saw-tooth bits. Bit sizes required are: 38 mm ($1\frac{1}{2}$ in), 25 mm (1 in), and 18 mm ($\frac{3}{4}$ in) for the best results for the mechanism being used. Set the depth stop to allow a 6 mm ($\frac{1}{4}$ in) recess to be cut in the base, gripping your wooden cylinder with a leather-faced glove to save your hand from being burnt if the drill grabs. Remove 38 mm ($1\frac{1}{2}$ in) drill and fit the 25 mm (1 in) in the chuck, depth set to drill 12 mm ($\frac{1}{2}$ in) deep in the base recess. Turn your cylinder over and drill centrally down to within 6 to 9 mm ($\frac{1}{4}$ to $\frac{3}{8}$ in) of connecting the two holes through. Remove the 25 mm (1 in) drill, fit the 18 mm ($\frac{3}{4}$ in) drill and connect the holes through, thus creating a step for the stator to rest on, allowing the peppercorns to pass through to be ground. Back to the lathe and mount between centres. A tapered wooden plug should be inserted in the base, and a revolving centre at the tailstock end should locate in the entrance hole at the top. True any slight inaccuracy at either end with a parting tool, set a pair of calipers to 54 mm ($2\frac{1}{8}$ in) and skew-chisel your cylinder true.

Now you are ready to design your base. It will be best if the first shaping from the bottom

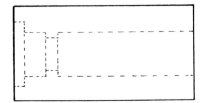

170 Sequence of holes drilled in the mill base.

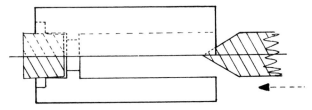

171 Body mounted between centres, showing plug and revolving centre.

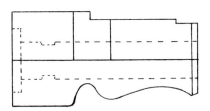

172 Top: the body reduced in stages with the feature lines marked; bottom: the final shape.

is not dimensionally less than the height of the knob you have to turn. This is one of the stages of getting proportion right. The knob will end up something in the region of 35 mm ($1\frac{3}{8}$ in) in length, so first shaping of the base should not start lower. Mark with a pencil the first design feature. The next line should be where possibly the most important surface change takes place,

for you will work upward and downward from it. A reduction in size by 6 mm ($\frac{1}{4}$ in) at this point will start to improve balance, as will a further reduction near the top of another 6 mm ($\frac{1}{4}$ in). Check both these diameters with calipers. You should now have a three-step type of cylinder. Shaping is now carried out between these points with gouges and chisels to obtain the desired form. Sand, oil, polish and remove from lathe.

Now to the knob. Mount the 25 mm (1 in) spigot in the appropriate chuck and turn another spigot just the same at the open end. Push an 8 mm ($\frac{5}{16}$ in) drill into the centre, 18 mm ($\frac{3}{4}$ in) or so deep. Check that the spigot will enter the base and mark with a pencil the

173 The finished base of a 152 mm (6 in) pepper mill.

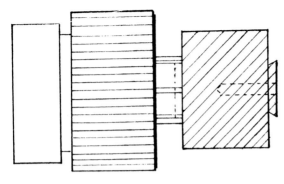

174 Knob mounted in the spigot chuck with the other spigot formed.

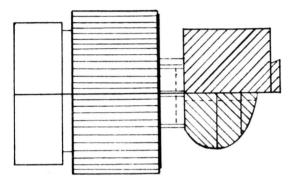

175 Knob remounted and turned to conclusion.

diameter of the base's top or the knob end. Remove from the chuck and turn round, fit the stator in the base, and push the mechanism stem through. Measure the protruding stem at the top of the base to determine the height of the knob. This should be about 35 mm ($1\frac{3}{8}$ in). Mark these dimensions from the knob and part off the surplus material. Reduce the size of the knob by 3 mm ($\frac{1}{8}$ in) smaller than the base's largest diameter and shape with the gouge and chisel between the guidelines, creating a soft knob. Take an 8 mm ($\frac{5}{16}$ in) drill and connect the hole in the centre through. Sand, oil, polish, and remove from the chuck. Fit up the necessary parts. Now you should have a well-balanced mill that looks good and feels right in the hand. Soft shapes always fit the hand best and seem more pleasurable to use. Harder-lined forms always look visually satisfying but seem less comfortable in use. The knob size on the taller mills should increase in length but should not exceed 50 mm (2 in), as this would make it difficult to achieve a bulbous effect. Lathe speed for carrying out all processes is around 1,400–1,500 r.p.m.

176 Finished 152 mm (6 in) mill knob.

177 A finished selection of mills.

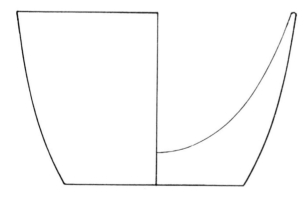

178 Drastic example of poor form unfortunately not uncommon.

Salad bowls

Bowls of all sorts are perhaps one of the face-plate turner's most produced items, yet they often are one of his least successful, particularly with regard to the design of salad bowls. The bowls will hold salad, certainly, but so will anything that has an open top, some depth and a bottom. Many bowls lack any form or sense of balanced shape, remaining simply a block of wood with a depression in it. Some look as though they would be impossible to remove from the table, so firmly attached do they look. Bases are often so thick that the bowl's holding capacity is cut by a quarter or more: the culmination of both poor design and poor workmanship.

It should be possible to design many shapes that are both functionally practical and also possess life and style. Let us consider a few of the *do's* and *dont's*. Anything less than 100 mm (4 in) in height can hardly be described as a salad bowl, unless it is a small individual one

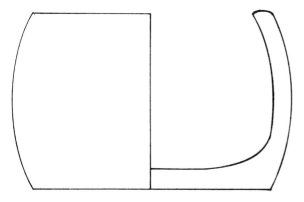

179 Central belly showing the lifeless form created.

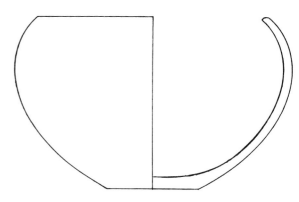

182 Again a good form, incurved with a base size of one-third of the diameter.

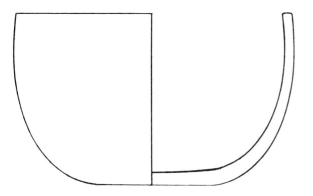

180 Bowl of improved proportions; the base is almost half of the maximum diameter.

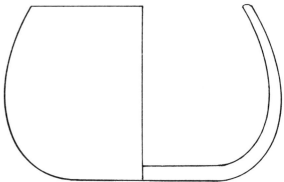

183 Variation of the incurved form but with the base more than half the diameter.

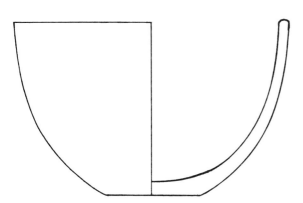

181 Good form, with base one-third of the maximum diameter.

for a side-salad. So height should be from 100 mm (4 in) upward. Base size is important both from the design and the stability point of view: less than one-third of the bowl's greatest diameter will result in poor stability, whereas more than two-thirds will make it difficult to design a shape that has life. Base sizes are best varied between these guidelines when creating any bowl shape for salad use. Another major *don't*, and perhaps the most important, is never to have the belly of the bowl equidistant between the base and top, for this will produce a surprisingly dull shape. The movement of any curves from the centre towards the top or the base will instantly start to give the bowl form. It is up to the turner's eye and ability to create pleasing shapes, once these principles have been grasped. If you take a look around the shops at salad bowls you will find that most are of an open form, rather than incurved or

95

184 Constant wall thickness, showing how the strength is improved through a curved arc.

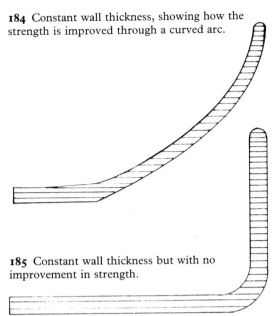

185 Constant wall thickness but with no improvement in strength.

straight-sided. There are several reasons for this. One is they are quicker and easier to make, but there is also an advantage in strength, enabling the bowl to stand up to knocks better.

Figs 184–185 show how a curved shape with a constant 12 mm ($\frac{1}{2}$ in) wall thickness will be superior in strength. The grain direction, being horizontal to the base, will at times lengthen through the curve of the arc to as much as 18 mm ($\frac{3}{4}$ in), whereas in a straight-sided bowl the grain strength will not increase over the wall thickness of the bowl. Any knock on the end grain makes it more susceptible to damage. It is worth remembering that curved shapes are always stronger than straight ones.

The timbers to be used are a matter of personal choice, but ash and elm are good

186 Shaping the outside of a large salad bowl with a 12 mm ($\frac{1}{2}$ in) high-speed steel bowl gouge.

Quilted paldao platter,
368 mm (14½ in) dia.

Below Shaped cocobolo bowls
and box. Largest bowl 120 mm
(4¾ in) dia. x 100 mm (4 in)
high.

Two wet-turned natural-topped rippled pear bowls, 140 mm (5½ in) dia. x 100 mm (4 in) high, with the log from which they were cut.

Natural-topped African blackwood bowl, 115 mm (4½ in) dia. x 90 mm (3½ in) high.

Natural-topped burr mulberry bowl, 203 mm (8 in) dia. x 127 mm (5 in) high.

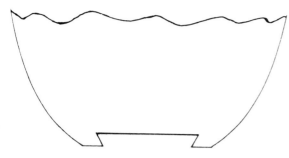

187 Recess formed in the base to accept the precision expanding collet.

native ones. These can normally be found in thick sizes. Methods of production again depend on personal preference, but I will explain my own here.

If the timber is dry, then it is a straightforward exercise. Mount on a face plate, turn the outside first with a 12 mm (½ in) high-speed steel bowl gouge. Commence cutting from the base towards the top. Try to stand at the lathe in a way that will allow all cutting to take place without the need to move the feet. In other words, the bulk of the body weight is over the right foot when starting to cut from the base. This will allow the whole body to sway gently from the ankles, transferring the weight on to the left foot as you reach the top of the bowl. The advantage of this method is that it affords a continuous fluid cutting movement without the need to reposition the feet. Repositioning inevitably leads to broken, stepped and rippled toolwork and results in surfaces which show the lack of fluid spontaneity. At all times aim for fluid movements rather than broken jerky ones. Correct positioning of the feet and body-

188 The interior being hollowed with the same gouge, the angle of which is 60°–65°.

189 Selection of ash salad bowls.

weight distribution will increase your chances of succeeding in everything you tackle in the lathe.

I have always found the use of a bowl gouge with 60–65° successful using these methods. Continue cutting with the gouge until you arrive at your desired shape. Most of the salad bowls I make have their interiors hollowed out while mounted on the precision combination chuck; in the expanding collet bowls up to 400 mm (16 in) diameter are made in this manner. True up the bowl base and mark the diameter of the collet you are going to use – larger collets for larger bowls, and vice versa. With a parting tool go in about 6 mm ($\frac{1}{4}$ in) deep on the inscribed line, remove material in the centre with the gouge and scrape true with a square-ended scraper. Undercut the required dovetail effect with a diamond-point scraper. Finally, lightly scrape the outside of the bowl with a square-ended scraper, preferably the heavy high-speed steel variety. Power-sand with 75 mm (3 in) Velcro (touch-and-close fastener) discs from 120 to 400 grit and oil-finish. Remove from the lathe and rechuck on the expanding collet. A hole in the centre of the bowl will make hollowing out easier, as mentioned with the mortar and sugar bowls. Hollow out with a 12 mm ($\frac{1}{2}$ in) high-speed steel bowl gouge with the 60–65° angle, cutting from the top towards the middle of the base, and aiming for a constant wall thickness throughout. The base thickness can be a little heavier by 3 mm ($\frac{1}{8}$ in) or so. Employing the balanced pivot positions, as described earlier,

with continuous cutting from the top to the base, the use of the short bevelled gouge will allow you to operate without the tool being less than 10–15° out of horizontal throughout, with the bevel rubbing just behind the cutting edge. Remove any ripples with light cuts from a heavy scraper, the shape of which depends on the form you have created. Finally power-sand and oil-finish. Bowl wall thicknesses depend on personal preference, but 9 mm ($\frac{3}{8}$ in) for a 250 mm × 100 mm (10 in × 4 in) is about right, going up to 15 mm ($\frac{5}{8}$ in) for a 450 mm × 150 mm (18 in × 6 in). Lathe speeds of around 800 r.p.m. are best up to 350 mm (14 in) or so, down to 425 r.p.m. for larger.

Bowls of the latter sizes are best made from unseasoned wood, making it easier to remove their bulk. Distortion is, of course, going to take place, so rough-turn these items, leaving enough material to true them up after they have dried out. Little shrinkage, if any, will take place in the length direction of the grain, but quite a lot will occur across the width. Most timbers will work well, used in this way; some better than others. If you have doubts about end-splitting, seal the ends and dry slowly.

Weigh the bowls when you rough them out and check-weigh them every two weeks or so. At the end of three months they should be completely dry. As a guide to wall thicknesses at roughing stage, for a 250 mm × 100 mm (10 in × 4 in) bowl leave not less than 18 mm ($\frac{3}{4}$ in). Up to 450 mm × 150 mm (18 in × 6 in) a wall thickness of 31 mm ($1\frac{1}{4}$ in) will be necessary. The use of PEG will stop the oval shrinkage, but I have passed comment on this solution in Chapter 12.

15 Individual items

When producing work of this nature, you need clear ideas of your aims for each piece. Consider what makes an individual piece. My own views are fairly straightforward. There should be a very strong emphasis on aesthetic appeal. Function is of secondary importance. My reasoning for this is that in most cases, where function starts to be considered, a compromise in form creeps in and the object usually fails on both accounts: being less functional and lacking the aesthetic elegance that was hoped for at the beginning.

This is a difficult problem for any maker to surmount in this country. Our traditions and the conservatism of the buying public tend to drive craftsmen to compromise. Any object that bears no relationship to an instantly recognizable form is viewed with suspicion, so most of us produce items that are refined versions of recognizable objects. Given these restraints, which we have to accept if we want to eat, the trick is then to make objects that display the minimum of compromise within these limitations.

The bowl possibly offers the widest range of challenges, but even here our problems are not over. A bowl which is designed primarily as an art object seems to demand justification for purchase in the eyes of the customer ('I suppose I could put nuts in it').

The term 'individual item' is open to interpretation. You may feel that any object made from a beautifully grained, figured or rare piece of wood fits the description. Here I disagree, for form is equally or more important. Or you may feel that form on its own is enough. Again I disagree, although I have more sympathy with this view. For me, it is the use of beautiful timbers combined with elegant, aesthetic form that makes a truly individual piece.

A good maker who deals with bland, predictable timbers should be able to produce on a regular basis objects that display well-designed aesthetic form, once he has arrived at a successful conclusion. There will, of course, be variations, as with anything hand-made, and some items will be more successful than others. The maker who relies on the timber's grain figure and forgets about form is doing himself, the public and the material a great disservice. It would be interesting to paint one of his pieces black or white all over and then stand back and take in the form, or lack of it.

The maker who possesses the ability to use timbers of real beauty and enhance them within elegant forms is really achieving his aims. A good test is to imagine the item you are making has no grain-figured beauty and just look at its form. In this way you will see whether you are getting close to your objectives. When dealing with timbers that have real inherent beauty, the maker must have a more flexible approach to his designs, exploring possible shapes in his mind for those he feels will accentuate nature's beauty through good form.

Throughout the search for these ideals the craftsmanship should be of the highest quality, for a good design that is poorly made is unsuccessful (so, by the same token, is poor design with superb craftsmanship). The maker who possesses the skills and the eye to design aesthetic forms that enhance nature's beauty, together with craftsmanship of the highest quality, is the most likely to reach regular successful conclusions.

Boxes

Boxes are normally containers to keep things in and so have a definite function; however, the approach to making boxes described here has been taken primarily from the aesthetic and craftsmanship viewpoint. The boxes can, of course, be used if necessary, but I know most are purchased for display. No doubt at the back of the mind of the purchaser, however, there is the thought that if challenged with 'What have you bought that for?' they can say the box is to keep pills or rings in.

For me, great pleasure is derived from making these objects without the feeling of compromise, for their small size allows me to work in a wide range of exotic timbers, all of which have different characteristics and beauties to exploit. If only one or two timbers were used it might prove difficult to keep one's interest, but a variety allows the woodturner to design aesthetic forms that enhance nature's beauty, with a need for craftsmanship of the highest standard.

What makes a good box? For me, it should be of a well-designed, balanced form, revealing nature's beauty to the full, through shapes that often possess a strong tactile appeal. The grain should match throughout the piece, the inside form should follow the contours of the outside wherever possible, and the craftsmanship should be of the same standard both inside and out. The lid should fit and should not fall off when the box is turned upside down. Best results will be achieved by using close-grained hardwoods that are as dry as possible. Moist timber will eventually result in a loose, ill-fitting lid.

Methods and proportions

To explain what happens when using a range of different forms, a piece of Brazilian tulipwood has been selected, for with its light and dark variegations, these effects are highlighted. Proportional height relative to diameter plays a significant part in the size of your object.

For this sequence all will be made from a 51 mm (2 in) square turned to a cylinder. Over the years I have found that lengths of 140 mm × 51 mm ($5\frac{1}{2}$ in × 2 in) diameter will yield two boxes of balanced shape when made in a three-jaw or spigot chuck, or sometimes a combined use of the two. Anything longer of this diameter held in these chucks can result in problems, for when hollowing on the end a tremendous leverage can be exerted. Boxes that

190 Indian rosewood finial box 85 mm ($3\frac{3}{8}$ in) high.

are knobbed, such as the finial one shown in Fig. 190, are best made singly, with an allowance in length made accordingly: 102–108 mm (4–$4\frac{1}{4}$ in) should be fine. After marking the centres of the squares and rough-turning into cylinders with a 31 mm ($1\frac{1}{4}$ in) roughing gouge, part both ends slightly concave as this will give stability when being held in the three-jaw. While between centres the cylinder to be used for the finial-type box is best prepared for mounting in the spigot chuck. My preference is for the use of the 25 mm (1 in) one, not the 38 mm ($1\frac{1}{2}$ in) one, as the base of the box will be small and access and strength will be more compatible for your needs. The spigot is best formed with a 9 mm ($\frac{3}{8}$ in) beading tool. Set a pair of calipers to 25 mm (1 in) and part in creating a spigot 3 mm ($\frac{1}{8}$ in) in length, then slightly undercut to allow maximum grip for the chuck. Mount one of your cylinders in the three-jaw chuck. All

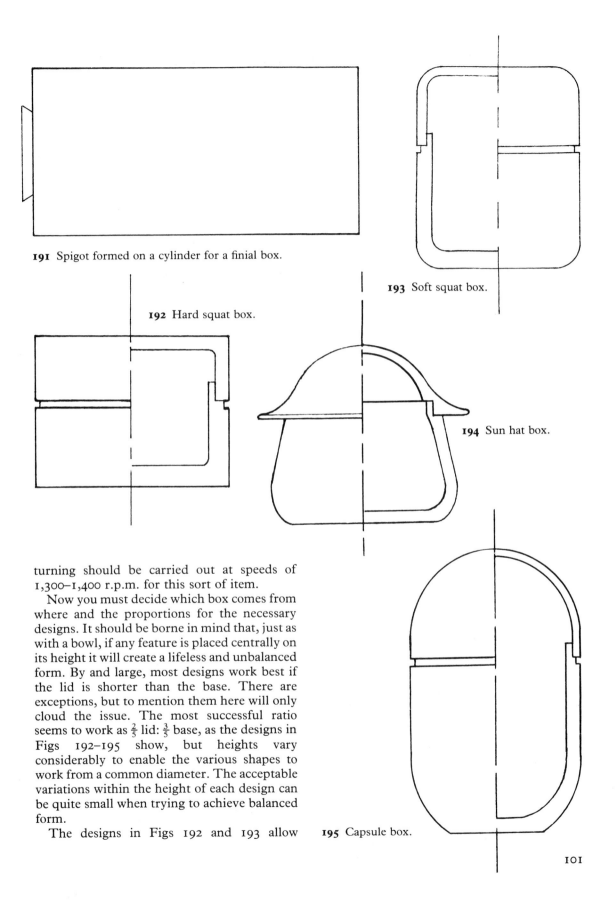

191 Spigot formed on a cylinder for a finial box.

193 Soft squat box.

192 Hard squat box.

194 Sun hat box.

turning should be carried out at speeds of 1,300–1,400 r.p.m. for this sort of item.

Now you must decide which box comes from where and the proportions for the necessary designs. It should be borne in mind that, just as with a bowl, if any feature is placed centrally on its height it will create a lifeless and unbalanced form. By and large, most designs work best if the lid is shorter than the base. There are exceptions, but to mention them here will only cloud the issue. The most successful ratio seems to work as $\frac{2}{5}$ lid: $\frac{3}{5}$ base, as the designs in Figs 192–195 show, but heights vary considerably to enable the various shapes to work from a common diameter. The acceptable variations within the height of each design can be quite small when trying to achieve balanced form.

The designs in Figs 192 and 193 allow

195 Capsule box.

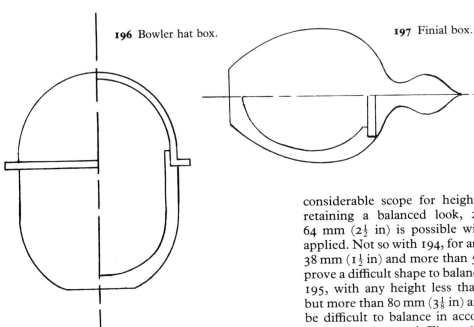

196 Bowler hat box.

197 Finial box.

considerable scope for height variance. Still retaining a balanced look, 25 mm (1 in) to 64 mm ($2\frac{1}{2}$ in) is possible with the $\frac{2}{5}:\frac{3}{5}$ ratio applied. Not so with 194, for anything less than 38 mm ($1\frac{1}{2}$ in) and more than 51 mm (2 in) will prove a difficult shape to balance. Again, that in 195, with any height less than 68 mm ($2\frac{5}{8}$ in) but more than 80 mm ($3\frac{1}{8}$ in) and the shape will be difficult to balance in accordance with the diameter being used. Fig. 196 almost gives the lie to the central feature theory, for in this case the lid forms $\frac{4}{9}$ and the base $\frac{5}{9}$. It also has the most critical height-to-diameter ratio, for anything less than 57 mm ($2\frac{1}{4}$ in) and more than 65 mm ($2\frac{9}{16}$ in) will almost certainly result in an unbalanced form. The box in Fig. 197 has the

198 Cylinder in the three-jaw chuck with the lid almost parted off for box in Fig. 192.

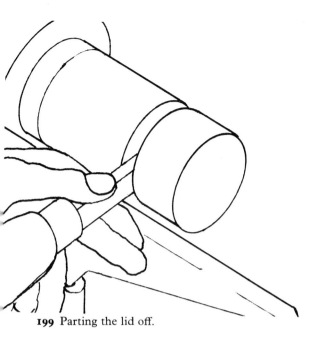

199 Parting the lid off.

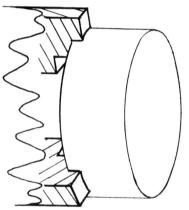

200 Lid mounted in three-jaw chuck.

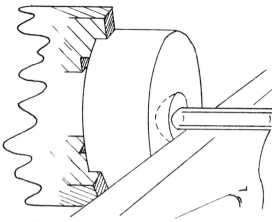

201 Hollowing with the gouge.

longest body-to-lid difference, for $\frac{2}{3}$ make up the body and $\frac{1}{3}$ the lid. Again the diameter-to-height ratio is quite tight: 6–8 mm ($\frac{1}{4}$–$\frac{5}{16}$ in) variance is all that is tolerable. All these height dimensions are based on diameters of 48–51 mm ($1\frac{7}{8}$–2 in) and any reduction or increase in diameter size will result in necessary height adjustments to balance the form.

As an exercise, the box in Fig. 192 will prove the simplest to produce. True up one end of your cylinder with a parting tool, removing any drive centre marks. Now mark out the various proportions with a pencil. In this case an overall finished height of 51 mm (2 in) has been decided on, so a line 20 mm ($\frac{3}{4}$ in) from the top gives the $\frac{2}{5}$ ratio lid. In theory you may think that a line 31 mm ($1\frac{1}{4}$ in) marked on the cylinder below this gives the base length, but an allowance has to be made for the waste of the parting tool width in removing the lid, plus the length of the spigot that will give a friction-held lid. In all, this adds up to 9–10 mm ($\frac{3}{8}$ in) if you use a 3 mm ($\frac{1}{8}$ in) high-speed steel parting tool. You will be left with 6–7 mm ($\frac{1}{4}$ in) to form your spigot. This length should never be shorter than 5 mm ($\frac{3}{16}$ in) on any box if you want a well-fitting lid. Having made the necessary allowances, part off the lid, remove the cylinder from the three-jaw chuck and mount the lid in the jaws with top trued surface inverted to rest on the jaws. This will eventually result in the grain matching through. True up the surface before starting to hollow out. This is best done with a 9 mm ($\frac{3}{8}$ in) high-speed steel spindle gouge with the short bowl bevel. Finally, true up with a square-ended scraper, if you wish. Set a depth gauge to leave 3–4 mm ($\frac{1}{8}$ in) thickness at the lid's top. Start to hollow the lid just as in making a salt bowl, i.e. present the gouge to the centre of the lid on your rest, just below centre height, with the open face towards you, horizontal to the bed. Tilt the face of the gouge away from you some 10–15° out of vertical. Now push in towards the headstock. You will find it acts like a drill. Make sure you do not go too deep; check with the depth gauge. Now open up the lid from the centre hole with a series of cuts aiming for a lid wall thickness of 3–4 mm ($\frac{1}{8}$ in). You will find

OPPOSITE
202 9 mm ($\frac{3}{8}$ in) high-speed steel spindle gouge ground with a 60°–65° bevel angle hollowing out the lid.

OPPOSITE BELOW
203 Scraping the lid inside with a square-ended side-cutting scraper.

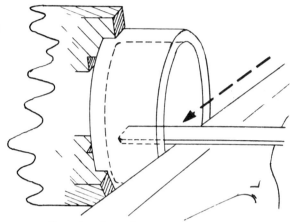

204 Scraping from the centre outwards.

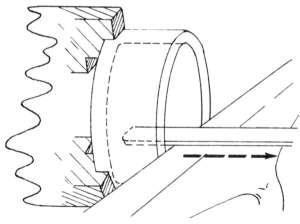

205 Pulling the scraper towards you up the lid side.

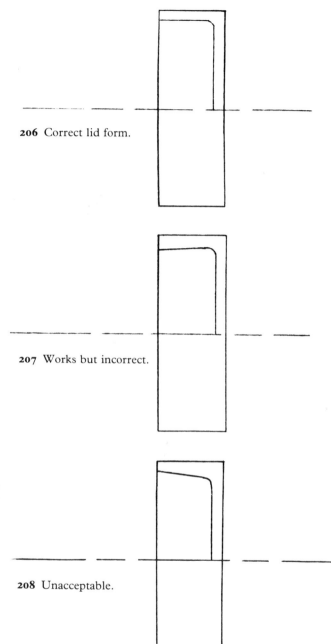

206 Correct lid form.

207 Works but incorrect.

208 Unacceptable.

the short bevel allows it to rub during most of the hollowing process. With a small scraper, 18 mm ($\frac{3}{4}$ in) wide, with a cutting edge on the end and side with a 4–5 mm ($\frac{3}{16}$ in) radius on one corner, true up your gouge marks in the bottom of the lid and side by moving the tool from the centre outwards and drawing the tool towards you up the inside lid wall.

It is important that the sides should be square. If in doubt, slightly undercut. Never taper inward, for it will be impossible to get a good lid fit to base. Sand and finish in your preferred way, but be careful not to soften the edge with excessive sanding. Remove from the chuck and remount the base cylinder. Take a parting tool and start to cut a spigot for the lid

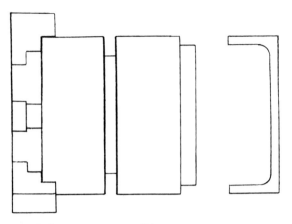

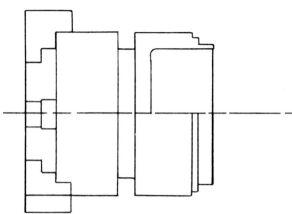

209 Spigot cut to accept lid.

212 Base hollowed out in the same manner as the lid.

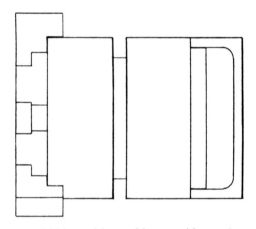

210 Lid in position and box outside trued up.

to fit on. This should end up 5–6 mm($\frac{3}{16}$–$\frac{1}{4}$ in) in length. Do not cut the full length at first, just in case you go too small. Constantly check with the lid to see that this does not happen. Although calipers will give a guide, the tight, snug fit you are looking for is an almost unmeasurable one. Once you have achieved the fit required, lengthen the spigot, which should remain parallel throughout its length, fit the lid and true the outside with a skew chisel. Mark the base length from the joint 30–31 mm ($1\frac{7}{32}$ in) and part in a short way. True the top with very light cuts with a square-ended sharp scraper. Remove the lid and before starting to hollow cut a little gap line about 2 mm ($\frac{1}{16}$ in) wide, 1 mm ($\frac{1}{32}$ in) deep. The point of this is that it takes the eye through any grain mismatch caused by the 10 mm ($\frac{3}{8}$ in) removal which takes place in the parting and creation of the spigot. Also, however dry the material used, most boxes go slightly oval in time. This line prevents you seeing or feeling this slight mismatch if not aligned correctly.

Now hollow out the base exactly as you did the lid, but aim for a 5 mm ($\frac{3}{16}$ in) consistent wall and base thickness. This will give a 2 mm ($\frac{1}{16}$ in) spigot thickness. Replace the lid and sand the exterior. Remove the lid and sand the interior. Never sand the spigot, as this will make your lid loose. Seal and wax in your usual way. 180 grit should have been the maximum abrasive needed. Finish down to 400 grit, finally 0000 wire wool. Part off the base of the box from the cylinder. I normally disc-sand and polish but, if you wish, turn a spigot on a waste block of wood, making a good fit for the base to go over, then tool up and finish.

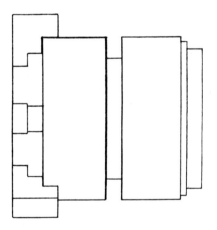

211 Lid removed and gap line created.

213 Box base being parted off with a 3 mm ($\frac{1}{8}$ in) high-speed parting tool.

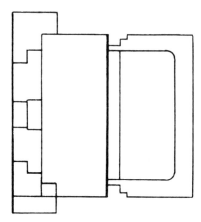

214 Base lid mounted on a waste block and trued up.

All the other boxes (Figs 192 to 196) are made using similar techniques and tools. There is, of course, more gouge and chisel work in the boxes shown in 195 and 196 and a side-cutting round-nosed scraper is also used on their insides. The box in 197 is different inasmuch as the lid is inset and is made without removing the body or rechucking the lid. Take the shorter cylinder with the pre-turned spigot and mount in the 25 mm (1 in) spigot chuck. In this case, the lid visually forms one-third of the box height, but as it is in-fitting, overall it is longer. We shall aim for a 30 mm ($1\frac{3}{16}$ in) lid length with a body of 60 mm ($2\frac{3}{8}$ in). Make the cylinder true with a gouge and pencil-mark a line some 35 mm ($1\frac{3}{8}$ in) from the unsupported end. Part in about 13 mm ($\frac{1}{2}$ in) behind this with the 3 mm ($\frac{1}{8}$ in) parting tool. Set a pair of calipers at 30 mm ($1\frac{3}{16}$ in) and reduce the knob part down to this size. Mark a pencil line 5–6 mm ($\frac{3}{16}$ in) up from the parting-tool cut. Now shape 95 per cent of the knob form with the 9 mm ($\frac{3}{8}$ in) high-speed steel spindle gouge before parting off. The most important part, however, is the 5–6 mm ($\frac{3}{16}$ in) shoulder. This should be parallel without taper in either direction, best

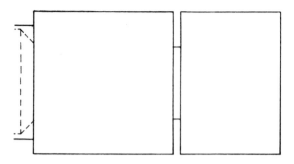

215 Cylinder parted for lid length.

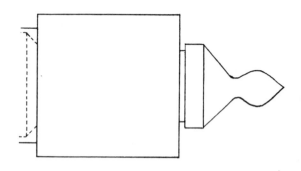

217 Lid/knob profile 95% formed.

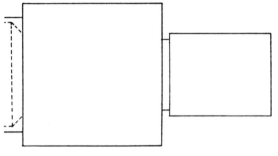

216 Lid/knob reduced to size.

218 Finial knob being formed with a 9 mm ($\frac{3}{8}$ in) high-speed steel spindle gouge.

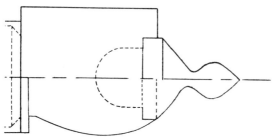

219 Top: body with lid fitted on shoulder; bottom: lid/knob blended into a threequarter-formed body.

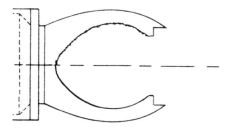

220 Top: the inside formed with the gouge; bottom: the inside after being scraped clean.

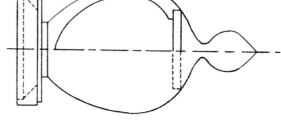

221 Box profile completed and ready for parting off.

achieved with the 9 mm ($\frac{3}{8}$ in) beading tool, used in the manner of a skew. Polish this part at this stage, for it is the only chance you get. Part the knob off, carefully sand the base on the disc and finally finish on 320 (wet and dry) paper and polish. Next turn a recess in the unshaped base cylinder. Mark the diameter of the lid on the end and start to open up as described in making Box (1). You need to form a shoulder for the lid to rest on about 5–6 mm ($\frac{3}{16}$ in deep) prior to completely turning the inside. Your aim is for a good tight fit so that when the lid is removed there is a suction 'pop' noise. This good friction fit is necessary to allow you to blend body and knob shape together. The shoulder is best formed with a small parting tool or diamond-point scraper. Check as you get close to size to ensure the good fit needed. When the lid is in place the shoulder should be slightly proud of the body at this stage. Now start to shape the outside of the base with the 9 mm ($\frac{3}{8}$ in) high-speed steel spindle gouge. At this stage, the aim is to create about three-quarters of the finished profile, successfully completing the blend of the base to lid and the top curves of the base. The profile towards the bottom of the box is purposely left thicker at

this stage to give strength while the inside is hollowed out.

Remove the lid and hollow as described in making the box shown in Fig. 192; set the depth gauge 8 mm ($\frac{5}{16}$ in) short of the spigot jaws to allow for a base of 5 mm ($\frac{3}{16}$ in) in thickness. You may find that the 6 mm ($\frac{1}{4}$ in) spindle gouge is best, as the inside is larger than the entrance. Careless use of tools inside can result in damage to the shoulder and entrance lip, so be careful. It is possible to create 95 per cent of the inside form with the gouge. The rounded side-cutting scraper will allow you to true up any ripples. With the rest set at the correct height, feed the scraper through the hole to the base and with careful manipulation gently draw it out towards you, removing gouge ripples on the way. The inside is now complete, apart from sanding. This is best left until final shaping of the outside has taken place.

Replace the lid. Part in with 3 mm ($\frac{1}{8}$ in) parting tool just above the spigot jaws and commence final shaping with gouge and chisel. If you prefer a scraper then you will need one with a longish angle. This will enable you to use the tool without fear of fouling on the chuck body. Remember though, cleaner results will be achieved with the chisel. Although the lid appears to have no part to play in this end sequence, its repositioning is most necessary as it enables you to decide the curves and base size needed to create a well-balanced form. All that is left to do is sand, polish and part off the base.

Through the various shapes shown, great visual changes take place using similar material. The box shown in Fig. 192 is fairly lifeless, with only the straight grain of the material showing. That in 193 starts to look a little more interesting, with the small curves

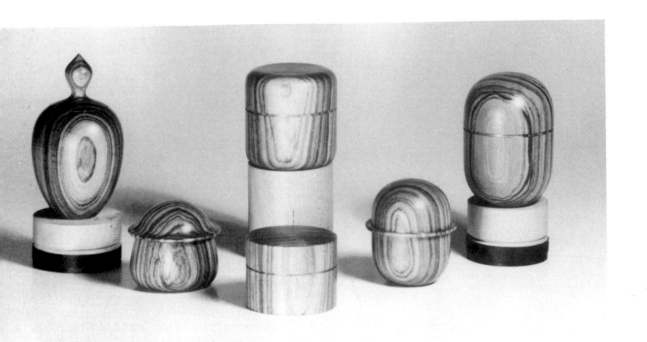

222 A finished group of the suggested designs in Brazilian tulipwood. Note how the shape changes affect the grain patterns.

223 A group of burred boxes. Left to right: birdseye maple, burr thuya, burr zebrawood. Largest 70 mm (2¾ in) high.

introduced either end. When we come to 194, we start to get much more interest, for the light and dark variegations follow the outside contour faithfully, becoming, in fact, a continuous reflective image, just as do the designs in 195 and 196. This gives the piece interest and life, but it also highlights any design fault, for a wrong curve is reflected many times over, magnifying the mistake.

When dealing with soft shapes in strong-grained timber, it is very important to get the shape right. The design in Fig. 197 again displays these qualities but has great variation in form. The others reflect an even shape top and bottom. The proportions of 197 are perhaps the most critical. If the knobbed lid is made too small it looks pimple-like, but if too large it dominates the base.

224 Soft knobbed boxes. Left to right: Mexican rosewood, Indian rosewood, cocobolo. Largest 82 mm ($3\frac{1}{4}$ in) high.

225 Finial boxes. Left to right: Brazilian tulipwood, Indian rosewood, Indian ebony. Largest 85 mm ($3\frac{3}{8}$ in) high.

Platters

These provide the turner with the equivalent of a canvas to explore, as they are made from slim discs of wood. Thus they are one of the few items where function and real beauty can be combined without the feeling of compromise. This is due in part to the shallowness, for the variation of options is more limited, resulting in many functional designs working equally well when using timber with a real inherent beauty.

When buying boards or planks, areas of rippled, burred-crotch, quilted or stained marking can often be found on boards that are predominantly plain. This is where the maker with his foot in both camps, i.e. functional and one-off areas of work, can sometimes have the best of both worlds.

My own approach when this occurs is to first mark out the areas of real beauty, aiming for the largest possible size. I much prefer to obtain one large item that reveals the true splendour of the timber than to dilute it by trying to obtain two or more smaller ones. For me this represents a sort of sacrilege, although from the sales viewpoint it will prove easier to sell the smaller ones. I remember admiring a large yew bowl of much beauty made by a fellow turner and asking if he had any more timber like it. 'Yes', he said, and went on to explain that he had cut it up for sugar bowls as the large bowl had not sold quickly. I considered this a near-criminal act of vandalism, for the real beauty of the wood could not be appreciated in such small items. That attitude is the one of the 'production' turner, as opposed to that of the maker who is always looking for material of beauty to use in the creation of objects with strong aesthetic appeal.

226 Crotch English walnut platter 380 mm (15 in) dia.

227 Quilted paldao platter 368 mm (14½ in) dia.　　**228** Rippled olive ash platter 356 mm (14 in) dia.

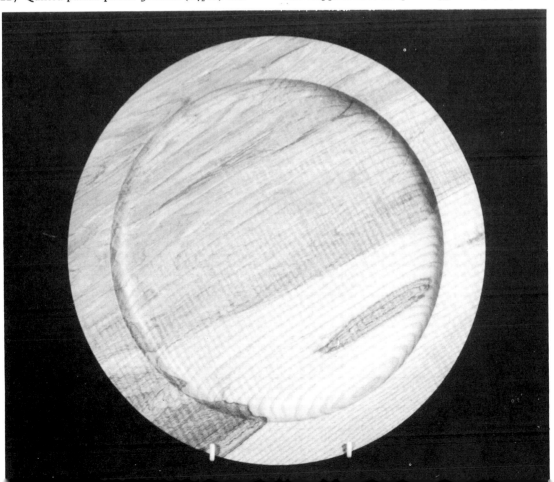

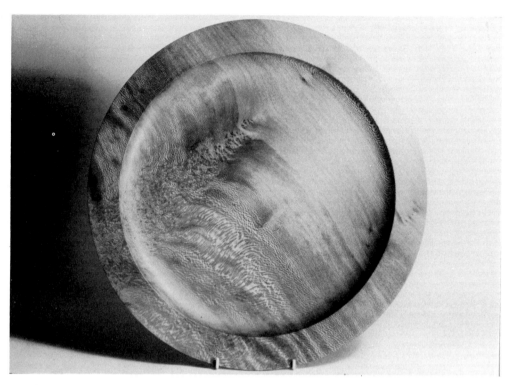

229 Quarter-sawn burred lacewood platter
432 mm (17 in) dia.

230 Plain goncalo alves platter with edge detail
254 mm (10 in) dia.

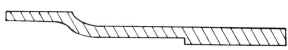

231 Top: a platter with convex interior and exterior; bottom: a platter with a thin flange tilted outward and heavy base.

The making of platters represents a fairly straightforward exercise for a competent face-plate turner, but it is amazing how few really good ones you see. I do not intend to explain the process of making but to give aims and objectives for balanced design.

The most common faults found in platters are these. Surfaces are often rippled and uneven, showing lack of care and control of the tools. The interiors and exteriors of surfaces are convexed. The base foot, if there is one, is too large or small, leaving a thick base with edges that are too thin and showing that the craftsman gave little thought to how he could bring out the best of the grain figure. These are some of the *dont's*. Now for some of the *do's*. The exterior is always turned first, whether the platter is to have a foot or not. The base should always be made slightly concave, allowing the largest diameter to rest on any surface. This will stop spinning or rocking. A platter with a foot is best balanced if the diameter is not smaller than $\frac{2}{5}$ of the overall size and not greater than half. Anything larger results in a lifeless piece and any smaller than the $\frac{2}{5}$ ratio makes the platter unbalanced. If a flange is to be used in the design, it should not be thinner than 4 mm ($\frac{5}{32}$ in, for any less makes it weak. The top surface of the flange should tilt inwards slightly towards the middle. Again, this helps to give life and poise. If it tilts outward or is exactly horizontal, the look of a soggy mushroom prevails. The interior surface should be at least flat or slightly concave, never convex, and any transitional curves well blended without rippled or uneven surfaces. Platters made from plainer timbers often benefit from some form of refined decoration near the outside. The photographs and drawings show some successful effects and designs.

232 Top: foot is too large; bottom: foot is too small.

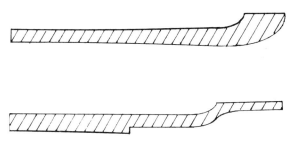

233 Top: similar design to Fig. 231 (top) but with surfaces slightly concave and the edge tilted inward; bottom: balanced foot size with edges tilted inward and surfaces slightly concave.

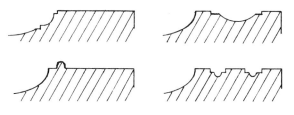

234 Edge profiles for plainer timbers.

Bowls

Individual bowl-making gives the turner one of the greatest areas of freedom to express his thoughts on shape and design, with the chance to use timbers of all sorts and sizes. From decayed wood that would not make a good fire to small, wet logs that are usually burnt, the opportunities are infinite, limited only by the maker's imagination and ability.

Throughout this section the emphasis will be on aesthetic form and the making of objects with an increasing degree of difficulty, incorporating nature's beauty. Several of the principles that apply to making bowls of function are disregarded, particularly the base-to-diameter ratio. My own objectives when

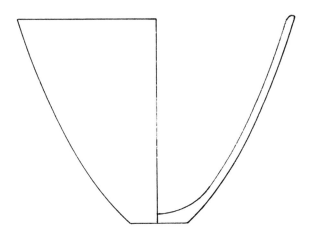

235 Thin-walled bowl with small base.

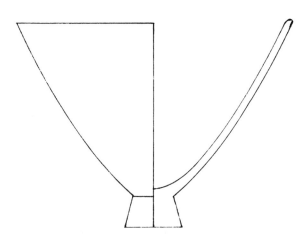

236 Thin-walled bowl with small foot.

areas. But my concern is for the craft of woodturning to be accorded a much higher level of appreciation and I feel the increased emphasis on artistry will help to achieve this.

The first move in creating a bowl that has aesthetic appeal is normally to turn something much thinner than would be practical for use, and frequently with a small foot or base. The combination of these two factors starts to give life to any bowl form. If the choice of wood and the way it is cut are also taken into account and the shape is designed to complement these factors, a pleasing decorative bowl should be

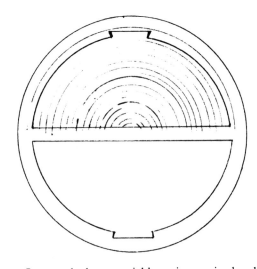

237 Log marked out to yield maximum size bowls.

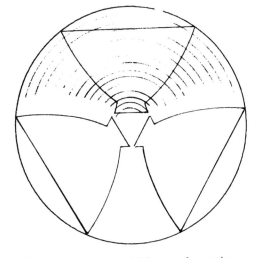

238 Log marked out to yield more decorative bowls, but creating more waste.

working in this area are to produce items that make a strong visual impact. This approach usually produces objects which are not functional, apart from giving great pleasure when touched or visually admired, but which display a strong artistic content. This is an area which always provokes heated discussions amongst craftsmen. The majority seem to feel that craft objects ought to be functional, yet where some of the leading exponents of crafts have chosen to produce art objects there has often resulted a far greater acceptance and credence from the public. This has given many craftsmen confidence to try new ideas so that the overall standard of the craft is raised, although many objects of extremely poor quality are still being produced in all craft achieved. The structure of the wood and the size of bowl have a considerable influence on the shape and design. If you are dealing with small bowls, say up to 203 mm (8 in) maximum diameter and around 102 mm (4 in) deep, really bold-grained timbers with wide growth rings can overpower the shape, for the size does not allow enough room for manoeuvre to take advantage of this feature. The size of log and the place where the timber is cut from within it make tremendous visual effect impact with bowls of similar shapes. The bowls in Figs 237–240 show exactly this, but the best use of the material has not been made. This has been done purposely in this instance to achieve the effect shown here. The bowls shown in 237 and 238 are made from a small cherry log some 165–178 mm (6½–7 in) in diameter. Cut in this way, it will yield two bowls 152 mm (6 in) by 76 mm (3 in) deep with the pith core boxed out, which is always preferable. Users of PEG will get away with leaving it in. The end visual effect of 237 is less attractive in my eyes than that achieved in Fig. 238. The problem with this is that there is a far greater wastage of wood. Three bowls will be possible but become much smaller; 114 mm (4½ in) diameter by 63 mm (2½ in) deep is about the best you can hope for. But the visual effect is more pleasing, as the grain figure gives an 'ovalling' effect through having cut through the growth rings.

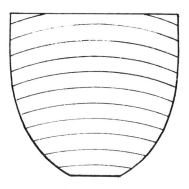

239 Bowl from large log through-sawn.

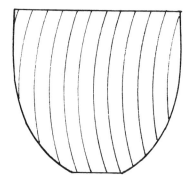

240 Bowl from large log quarter-sawn.

241 Cherry log marked out prior to cutting.

242 End-view photo of the bowls cut from the log in Fig. 241.

243 View looking into the same bowls, showing the tremendous visual effect difference.

You will note in both bowls that the sapwood has been incorporated. In a timber such as cherry it has little distinction in colour from the heartwood. This is true of most light-coloured timbers. In dark woods the contrast is much more pronounced, which can give added interest. In exotics, particularly, it can be very dramatic. Logs of the size used here will not work with a great many timbers. In pine, for instance, the sapwood could make up as much as 80–90 per cent of the log. At the other end of the scale, oak would be equally unsuccessful, although 70 per cent or more may be heartwood. Thoughts of using the sapwood here should be dismissed. Neither of these timbers are really turners' woods, especially for the type of items described. Also, if you intend to turn from seasoned timber, it would be a major achievement in itself to dry this type of wood without mass radial checking, even in our climate. Sapwood, by and large, is much softer than heartwood, and for this reason it is normally removed, as attacks by worm and decay are more likely. For the type of work engaged in here it is no major problem. The sapwood in exotic timbers is often just as hard as the heartwood and even if softer is normally harder than most northern-grown temperate

244 Side view of bowls cut from a 760 mm (2 ft 6 in) olive ash tree in different ways. Each is 152 mm (6 in) × 152 mm (6 in).

245 Bowls from Fig. 244, viewed from above.

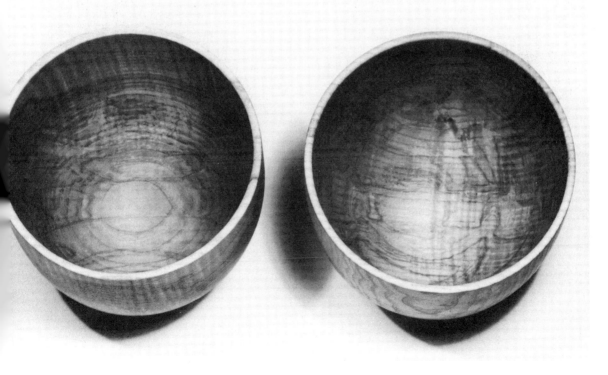

hardwoods. The bowls shown in Figs 239 and 240 are made from a rippled olive ash tree some 760 mm (2 ft 6 in) in diameter. The bowl in 239 was cut relative to the heart as 238, but the effect is dramatically different. The size of the log results in an almost horizontal, tiered layer effect of growth rings, similar to cutting through laminated veneers. The result is a constant reflection of the outside shape of ever increasing and decreasing diameters, depending on the way you look at it. Made as in 240, a totally different effect is created, being made in the quarter-sawn manner. The growth rings give a laminated veneer effect but this time vertically. For me, this is a far less pleasing effect but the rippled figure of the material is a saving grace.

Any item made from quarter-sawn timber will, in general, be much less prone to distortion, but is less visually satisfying. There are a few exceptions, such as oak or plane, but bowls of this nature would destroy their

246 Side view of bowl in Fig. 242.

247 Bowl from Fig. 242 being drum-sanded to shape. Note the gloves.

attractive characteristics. Flat surfaces make best use of their ray-fleck figure.

A closer look at the bowl from Fig. 242, viewed from the side in Fig. 246, shows the growth rings dipping down towards the base. It seems logical to try and reflect this feature by shaping the top, and this is something I often do. A pneumatic 180 mm (6 in) drum sander is used to create this effect. The bowl is hand-held and shaped by eye. This is where the leather-palmed gloves come in, to give a good grip. For really satisfactory results the bowl wall thickness must be constant, for any thickening is instantly shown up through the contours created. The edge will need to be softened after this; shaping, files and mild abrasives are my choice. Be careful not to damage your finished surfaces at this stage. The end product will certainly have taken on a considerably different form and will exhibit far more aesthetic appeal. An illusion of oval form is introduced through the edge's contour, reflecting that of the elliptical grain formation created throughout the bowl's shape.

Another more instantaneous creation of this illusion is by using the natural contour of the outside of any log or tree. Your skill in tool handling will have to be higher, for at times you will be turning in space. The need for steady and controlled handling of the tools becomes instantly apparent, especially when turning the inside.

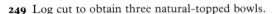

248 The end product after final hand-sanding on the edge.

249 Log cut to obtain three natural-topped bowls.

Maximum use of a small log is afforded when making bowls of this type. It will prove possible to cut three natural-topped bowls from one 165–178 mm (6½–7 in) log. These will finish up about 128 mm (5 in) in diameter and 70 mm (2¾ in) or so deep. The stages of this bowl's development are shown in Figs 249 to 254. All small logs can be used in this way. Sometimes with slow-grown and carefully seasoned ones the bark will remain and can be an extra attractive feature. Exotics being something of a forte of mine, I sometimes feel a sense of frustration that a great many of the logs shipped over have their sapwood adzed off, resulting in ragged and sometimes even jagged edges when turning bowls in this way. The net result is that some shaping has to be done on the drum sander to tidy things up. Those timbers that offer the most contrast between sapwood and heartwood will give the most striking effect.

A progression to more dramatic and challenging bowls often results when you get used to working in this way. A note of caution

250 Stage one before mounting in the lathe; bandsaw roughly round with hole for pin chuck in the centre.

251 Pin-chucked and shaped with foot for spigot chuck remounting.

252 Mounted in the spigot chuck prior to
hollowing.

253 The end product.

254 A group all from the same cherry log, showing the different results.

255 Two African blackwood bowls with natural tops. Note the dramatic sap-to-heartwood difference. The largest is 178 mm (7 in) dia. × 127 mm (5 in) high.

256 Indian ebony bowl with African blackwood box and bowl. Ebony bowl 150 mm (6 in) dia. × 100 mm (4 in) high.

257 Natural-topped burr elm bowls 150 mm (6 in) high × 100 mm (4 in) dia. and burr thuya box.

must be added here. Your skill needs to be very great when dealing with edges of varying heights. I remember turning a burr elm bowl once, some 255 mm (10 in) in diameter and 216 mm (8½ in) deep on one edge but only 102 mm (4 in) on the other. This, of course, resulted in intermittent cuts being taken on only one edge a good deal of the time as it revolved. Any slight lapse of concentration when dealing with such projects can be dangerous and disastrous. I did bruise one finger quite badly as I forgot for a split second that the spinning mass in the lathe didn't represent a continuous surface. Fortunately, no great harm resulted, but it served to remind me to have more respect and to keep my mind on what I was doing. Burred timbers can give some of the most dramatic and satisfying effects when creating bowls of this type.

258 Natural-topped burr box elder 165 mm (6½ in) dia. × 127 mm (5 in) high.

Because of their grain structure, most are best left with thicker walls than those previously described. An increase in size is also beneficial. The thicker edge shows more of the ragged points of the burr, all adding to the dramatic effect.

When buying burred logs it is worth remembering that often the characteristic figure does not go much deeper than its visual projection from the tree's trunk. There are, of course, exceptions. The burred oak log in Fig. 262 is a rare beast, and one I am very pleased to own. The burr figure on the end can be seen to go in at least 380 mm (15 in) towards the heart

259 Selection of burrs and natural-topped bowl blanks prepared for turning.

260 The end results of some of the blanks in Fig. 259.

all the way round. Looking down into a burred bowl from above, the bottom should be covered with those twig-bud eye formations, if it has been cut as the drawing shows.

Many other possibilities exist for using burrs. If the one in Fig. 263 was inverted a smooth-topped bowl would result, but the underneath could have the rugged outer-knobbed growth effect. A bowl made from a burr, cut with knobbly projections on the side, rather than top or bottom, will give its best visual effect when seen from the side. I could go on and on giving examples of effects and illusions that can be created by understanding and experiment, but there is only one way to really see what is possible and that is to try things for yourself. Every piece of timber is different and possibilities abound.

I have attempted to give some small insight into what is possible by applying a few basic

LEFT
261 A close-up of the elm bowl with a natural-formed foot, 150 mm (6 in) high × 133 mm (5¼ in) dia.

262 Burr oak log 1152 mm (60 in) dia. at the end.

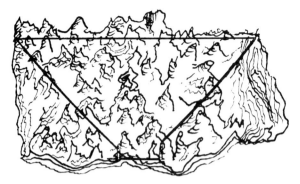

263 Typical burr section; this would show bud eyes.

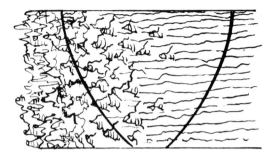

265 The burr used to show the bud eyes on the side.

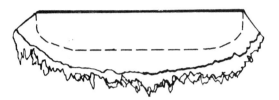

264 Inverted burr section, again possibly showing bud eyes.

266 Burr used to create a natural-topped bowl.

267 Burr thuya bowl turned from a burr, cut as in Fig. 265, 190 mm ($7\frac{1}{2}$ in) dia. × 120 mm ($4\frac{3}{4}$ in) high.

268 Large burr elm bowl showing the burr dying out towards the heartwood, 400 mm (16 in) dia. × 100 mm (4 in) high.

269 Small shaped translucent olivewood bowl, 2 mm ($\frac{1}{16}$ in) wall thickness.

principles. As to the choice of timbers, dense, close-grained varieties will give the most consistently successful results. Exotics are my favourites, and most prove ideal for the type of work described. Their fascination for me is their vast range of colours and different working characteristics, which always present constant challenges, from olive wood that cuts like butter and becomes translucent as you turn it thinner – the little bowl in Fig. 269 has a thickness of only 2 mm ($\frac{1}{16}$ in) – to African blackwood which is almost like cutting metal.

One of the most recent developments in turnery has been the creation of similar objects to those previously described, but in 'wet wood'. This technique was pioneered in the very late seventies by Jim Partridge and Richard Raffan. It is something I seldom do myself, for the timbers that work most successfully hold little appeal for me, being for the most part rather bland and white. There are now many other makers who work in this field. The term 'wet wood' means wood with the sap still in it. A tree cut yesterday can be used today, with none of the seasoning problems most of us subject ourselves to. It is a very instantaneous way of working. The wood,

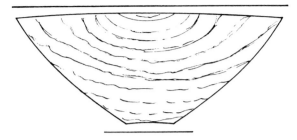

270 Wet-turned bowl with the centre core of the heart at the top edge: it is normal for the shrinkage to occur away from this as shown.

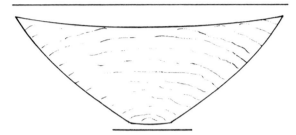

271 Wet-turned bowl showing the opposite reaction, with the core at the base. An ovalling effect will have taken place in each case when viewed from above.

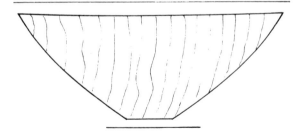

272 A wet-turned bowl quarter-sawn will have less distortion, but will also be less interesting.

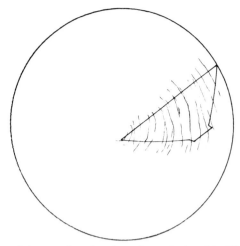

273 A log section showing where the bowl in Fig. 274 was cut from; a badly uneven shrinkage occurred.

being wet, will cut like butter, far more easily than any seasoned wood. There is so little resistance to tools that work can be turned at higher speeds, up to, say, 2,000 r.p.m. for a small holly bowl, whereas with something of similar size in African blackwood, any more than 800 r.p.m. would be hard to cope with. Because of the type of timbers normally used: holly, beech, sycamore, chestnut, and fruit woods, the fact that they have to be turned very thin to stop cracking has drawn more collectors to the craft. Many have been interested in porcelain and see in the light colours and thin forms a certain similarity. The maker must work fast and turn the wood thin, or during the drying process after making, the inevitable distortion and stresses will result in cracking. The makers I know who work in this field are very proficient craftsmen, and they need to be. Speed is of the essence, for as the bowls become thinner, distortion can take place during the making, and the longer you take the more the distortion. Subsequently, more are lost in the making stages. All the pieces will distort after turning, and this is where the proficient maker's work is lost, not in the lathe. Most will tell you that a loss factor of 25 per cent is an acceptable rate with this technique. This is caused by distortion that renders the pieces aesthetically unacceptable in the eye of the maker. On first trying this method losses will be even higher; some 50 per cent to 60 per cent is not uncommon. This loss factor may seem very high, but it must be remembered that it is possible to turn two or three such bowls for every exotic one, and material costs are negligible. It is an area of the craft that has a far too high a waste factor for my liking, as 2 per cent to 3 per cent is about my toleration point. If you do intend to work in this field, the need to understand what happens to wood when stresses are released will be of paramount

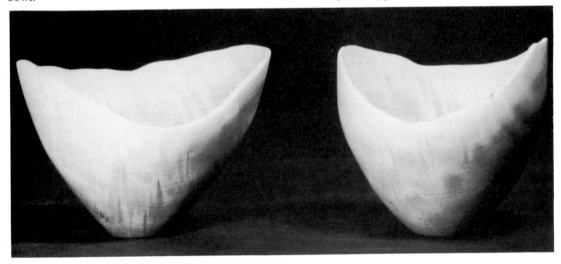

274 Badly distorted (wet-turned) figured holly bowl.

275 Natural-topped wet-turned rippled pear bowls, 140 mm ($5\frac{1}{2}$ in) dia. × 100 mm (4 in) high.

importance to help cut your waste factors. A guide is given in Figs 270 to 273. The common happening will almost certainly be an ovalling effect, for wood always shrinks less longitudinally.

Using wet woods when you are first learning to turn, not to produce any item but just for practice, may prove beneficial. A chunk from the log pile will cost little, and practice is what you need.

Shapes and methods

Throughout this discussion, little has been said about either, but here I will try and explain a few of the principles of each. I hope these will help you achieve more success, but however much anything is explained, the end result is down to you.

As indicated earlier, the material's grain formation should play an important part in the shape the bowl takes. Your aim is to enhance any real natural beauty through forms that will complement it.

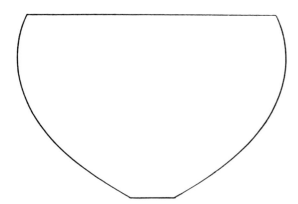

276 Bowl showing easy flowing curves.

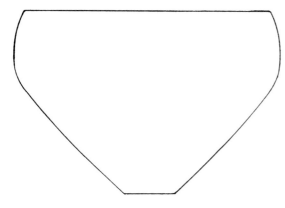

277 Bowl showing too flat a lower section curve in relationship to that in the upper section, resulting in an unbalanced piece.

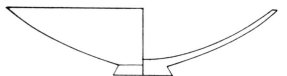

278 Open-dished bowl that would show off burrs to good effect.

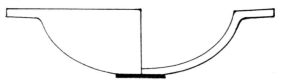

279 Open-flange bowl that works well with burrs, and also with figured quarter-sawn timber, as the flange shows this off to the full.

To give life to any bowl, the fullest curve should never be central, for this gives an extremely dull look. My own aims are always to create flowing curves through the piece. Any transitions from gentle to hard curves should flow evenly without flat or uneven areas creeping in, for these will destroy the smooth, elegant image you are aiming for. Any major fattening or hardening of curves should take place towards the top or bottom, as this will retain balance and life within the piece if done

280 Rippled olive ash dish 407 mm (16 in) dia.

well. It is virtually impossible to give the base-size diameters relative to height and top diameters to create balance of form, for much depends on the curves you create between these points, and the figure of the various timbers often calls for design modifications. Sometimes the resultant change of curve is too small to measure, whereas in others a major shift of emphasis is called for. With timbers such as burrs, where often the major beauty is going to appear in the base of the piece, the designs normally need to be broad-based or of open form to take full advantage of this feature. A bowl cut radially from a small log is best served by having a small base, thus exposing the oval ringing effects to the maximum. If surface directional changes are contemplated, then these should take place near the top or base of the bowl. If the major proportion of the shape is of convex form, then rather than just a flat shape change, a move to concave form should be considered, for greater emphasis.

The introduction of an incised line at the

281 Californian-grown English walnut, 230 mm (9$\frac{1}{16}$ in) dia. These bowls are not burred, but their shapes would be complimentary to most burred material.

point of surface change can lend an even stronger effect. Bowls that have a foot can often be the most difficult of all to bring to a successful conclusion. There are so many things to take into account, their height relative to diameter, their diameter relative to bowl size, whether they should be vertically parallel or taper inward at the top, and so on. Often the difference between success or failure is very small. Slightly large, and the bowl looks lifeless and heavy; too small and it is totally unbalanced.

The making of all the bowls suggested here will be successful only if you have become proficient in the use of the gouge. The ability to cut in a continuous controlled manner will increase your chances of success, coupled with

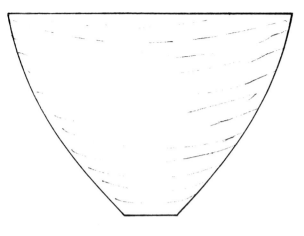

282 Small bowl, reflecting the growth rings.

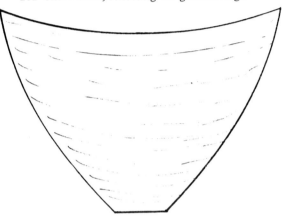

283 Similar to bowl in Fig. 282, but with the edge shaped, giving an added aesthetic appeal.

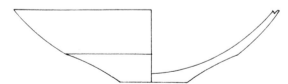

284 Concave curve near the base with an incised line.

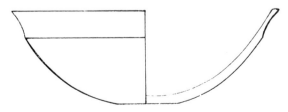

285 Concave curve near the top with an incised line.

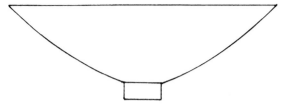

286 Simple bowl, parallel foot.

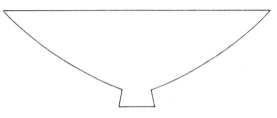

287 Simple bowl, tapered foot.

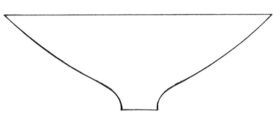

288 Simple bowl with flowing radius at the foot, perhaps resulting in the form with the most life.

289 The shaped top gives a more elegant form.

a good eye for form. The vast majority of the bowls suggested I have envisaged as between 2–4 mm ($\frac{1}{16}$–$\frac{5}{32}$ in) in wall thickness, except for the burrs, where 5–8 mm ($\frac{3}{16}$–$\frac{5}{16}$ in) becomes tolerable. This is for bowls up to 203 mm (8 in) in size. Over this, much heavier and chunkier bowls will work. Treated in the right way, these can give an image of power and rugged beauty.

Methods of mounting in the lathe depend on personal preference, but the vast majority of my own work is mounted on the pin or screw

290 Natural-edged bowls pre-drilled for pin chuck.

chucks, the outside always being at least part-turned first. The pin is the most versatile, for a central hole drilled in a natural log bowl makes for the easiest mounting of all. Many turners prefer to rough turn shapes like this between centres prior to using a three-jaw chuck for many of their future operations. Many of the small bowls can have their outsides completely turned and finished, and are usually rechucked in the 25 mm (1 in) or 38 mm (1½ in) spigot chucks for the hollowing of their interiors. When dealing with exotics this method is seldom used, for several reasons. Firstly, they are much heavier and denser, and often brittle. Then, as far greater resistance is encountered when hollowing, it is possible for the spigot to pinch off the base under the extra leverage. My normal procedure is to part-shape the outside and leave the base much wider than it will finish up. This will give support while the inside is shaped. The base is trued with gouge

and scraper, then sanding-disc trued. The roughness helps give a good surface on to which a small waste block may be glued; this is normally 19 mm (¾ in) birch plywood. When the glue has set it is rechucked on the pin, and the plywood face is made slightly concave. A centre hole for a screw chuck is created by pushing a suitable drill directly into the centre, supported by the tool rest. Another reason for using this method is that maximum possible use of the timber is afforded, as there is no need to part off spigots from the base.

Wet-turned bowls are often shaped in a series of chucking methods, mostly using the three-jaw and spigot chucks. After rough shape-turning, often done between centres, the base is mounted in the three-jaw and a great deal of weight is removed from the inside, but with an internal step created for the chuck to reposition on when the bowl is inverted over it. This done, final shaping of the outside can be carried out. Often a spigot mounting is created in the base for use with this chuck. The reason for removing a great deal of the inside is to allow for the spigot-chucking method. The fact

291 Pushing drill into the centre of a waste block.

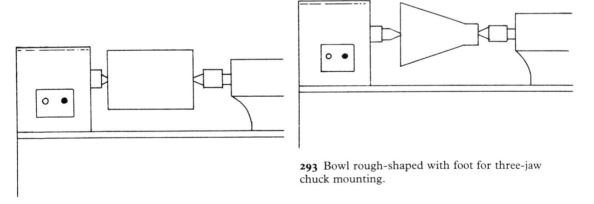

292 Bowl block mounted between centres.

293 Bowl rough-shaped with foot for three-jaw chuck mounting.

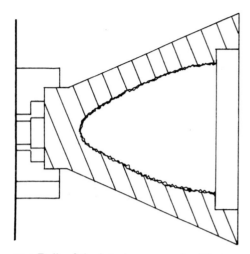

294 Bulk of the interior removed, with step created for the three-jaw.

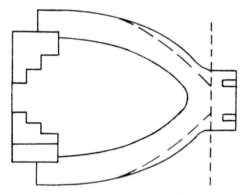

295 Rechucked bowl with the bulk of the outside formed and the spigot chuck recess created.

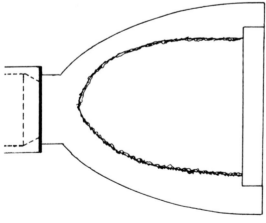

296 Rechucked on the spigot for final interior shaping.

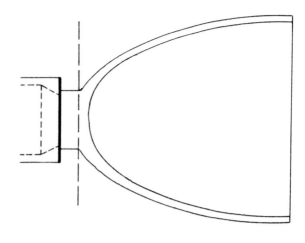

297 The end product. The base can be parted off, or a foot formed for a little more refinement.

that the wood is wet means the fibres compress more, and if removal of the inside's solid mass was attempted it could cause problems through the leverage that would be exerted. The hollowing of all bowls should be undertaken with gouges; 90–95 per cent of their interiors ought to be formed with them. You should find it possible with some of the small and wet bowls to achieve all shaping with gouges, if you have achieved mastery of their use. You are aiming to reflect the outside contour of the bowl. Constant wall thickness is your goal. A steady hand and eye are needed, backed by positive actions. To help achieve this, I have found the use of short bevelled gouges with angles of 60°–65° makes it possible for continuous sweeping cuts to be made in an almost horizontal plane from top edge to base. Different sizes of gouge will be needed for different timbers and sizes of bowl, but wet, burred and most northern temperate hardwoods will allow the use of a 13 mm ($\frac{1}{2}$ in) high-speed steel bowl gouge ground straight across. Exotics have far greater resistance when being cut than the woods just mentioned, so smaller ones work best: 9 mm ($\frac{3}{8}$ in) or sometimes 6 mm ($\frac{1}{4}$ in) ground to a fingernail shape but still with the short bevel. The fingers of the left hand are used to support the bowl's outside as it gets thinner, with just the thumb in contact with the gouge to act as a guide. When turning natural-topped bowls, draw back before the web of skin between index finger and thumb gets torn.

298 Natural-topped burr mulberry bowl ready for the interior to be shaped.

299 The 12 mm ($\frac{1}{2}$ in) high-speed steel bowl gouge hollowing with hand support.

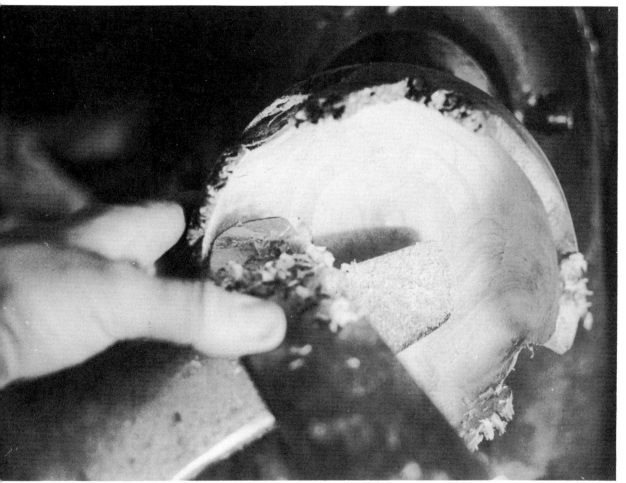

300 Scraper in use near the top with the hand supporting, before the bulk of material near the base has been removed.

You will find you need a scraper to true up bowls of the natural-topped variety. For much of the time your gouge will be in fresh air as the bowl rotates. This usually results in a few ripples near the top, as the gouge has no continuous surface for its bevel to rub on. The scraper should be used before the bulk of the timber is removed lower down, for the structure weakens with the removal of more wood. The risk of shattering will increase if scraping near the top is left till near the end.

Most exotic bowls with small bases are best turned in this way. A great deal of resistance will be encountered when hollowing out their interiors, because of their hardness, so it makes

sense to leave the base larger until this has been done. To give a guide for the correct form of the interior, two-thirds of the outside shape is created before this happens. The inside is completely turned and finished off before the final shaping of the outside is complete.

The bowl form must have been the most-produced object in the history of man, so it seems reasonable to conclude that many similar designs have been arrived at over the centuries. Given this thought, it is always going to be difficult to come up with something entirely original, so the best we can hope for is to develop a style that becomes identified as our own.

As a maker, nothing gives me greater pleasure than when someone tells me they can recognize my work anywhere, adding that they like what they have seen. That makes things really worth while.

301 The finished bowl, burr mulberry natural-topped, 203 mm (8 in) dia. × 127 mm (5 in) high.

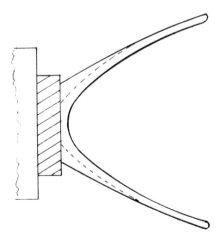

302 Exotic bowl on waste block with inside complete. Final outside shaping takes place after this, as the dotted line shows.

Suppliers

Turners' suppliers

Craft Supplies
The Mill
Millersdale
Buxton
Derbys SK17 8SN
Tel. 0298 871636

Craft Supplies USA
1644 S
State Street
Provo
Utah 84601
USA
Tel. (801) 373-0917
(USA distributor of the Harrison Graduate Lathe.)

Lathe manufacturers

Tyme Avon
Tyme Machines (Bristol) Ltd
Kings Wood
Bristol BS15 2JD
Tel. 0272 603726

Coronet Major
Coronet Tool Co (1982) Ltd
Alfreton Road
Derbys DE2 4AH
Tel. 0332 362141

Arundel K600
Treebridge Ltd
Mills Drive
Farndon Road
Newark
Notts NG24 2SN
Tel. 0636 702382

Harrison Graduate
T. S. Harrison & Sons Ltd
Union Street
Heckmondwike
West Yorks WF16 0HN
Tel. 0924 403751/6

Timber suppliers

North Heigham Sawmills
Paddock Street
Norwich NR2 4TW
Tel. 0603 22978
(Domestic and exotic.)

Rolston Timber
32 High Street
Keil Close
Broadway
Worcs
(Domestic and imported.)

Finishing materials

Fiddes & Son
Florence Works
Brindley Road
Cardiff CF1 7TX
WALES
Tel. 0222 40323

Index

abrasives
  garnet 54
  oxide aluminium 54
  silicon carbide (wet and dry) 54, 55
  Trimite 56
anglepoise lamp 48

band saw 28
bowls
  domestic
    mortar 73–7
    salad 94–8
    salt 77–82
    sugar 82–5
  aesthetic
    burred 126
    exotic 130, 136, 138
    natural-topped 121, 122
    shaped-topped 121, 125
    small base 116, 135
    small foot 116, 135
    wet 130, 131
boxes 99
  bowler hat 102
  capsule 101
  finial 100, 102, 107–10
  hard squat 101–7
  soft squat 101
  sun hat 101

calico mop 48
calipers
  inside 47
  outside 47
centre finder 48, 49
centres
  cone 45, 46
  four-prong 45, 46
  revolving 45, 46
  ring 45, 46
  two-prong 45, 46
chain saw 29, 31
chisels
  skew 32, 34, 52, 53
  square 32, 34

chucks
  conical friction 46
  cup or bell 42, 88
  Jacobs 46, 89
  pin 45, 135, 136
  precision combination 44, 45
  precision spigot 43, 44
  three-jaw 43, 100, 136

depth gauge 47, 48
designs
  individual items 99
    bowls 115–41
    boxes 99–111
    platters 112–15
  kitchen
    chopping board 70–73
    mortar and pestle 73–7
  tableware 68, 69, 77, 78
    pepper mills 89–94
    salad bowls 94–8
    salt bowl 78–82
    spoons 85–9
    sugar bowl 82–5
discs
  foam-backed 56
  sanding 28, 31
  Velcro (touch-and-close fastener) 56–8
dividers 47, 82
drills
  electric 28, 31
  pillar 28, 31
dust extractor 28–31

exotics
  buying 67
  faults 67
  using 130, 131, 138, 140

face mask 48
face plates 41, 42
files 40
finishes
  cellulose melamine 59
  oil 58

finishes—*continued*
  shellac 59
  waxes 59

gloves 48, 49, 120, 121
glue 48, 136
goggles 48, 49
gouges
  bowl 32, 33, 71, 75, 83
  long and strong 32
  roughing 32, 75
  spindle 32, 33, 72, 81, 87
  standard 32
grinder 28, 29
grinding 38–40

hopper hood 30, 31

lathes 23–7
  Arundel Treebridge K600 23, 25
  Coronet Major 23, 25
  Harrison Graduate 24, 26, 27
  Tyme Avon 23, 24

parting tools 34, 35
pencils 48
PEG 62, 63, 64, 117

rings, face-plate 45
router 28, 86, 87
ruler, steel 48

safety 40
sanding
  belt 31
  disc 28, 31
  drum 120, 121
  hand 54–6
  power 56–8
scrapers 35–7
  diamond-point 36
  long-angled 36, 109

round-nosed 36
side-cutting round-nosed 36, 109
side-cutting square 35, 105
square-ended 36
sharpening 38–40
sizing tool 48
smock 48
stance 50, 51

timber buying 60, 63, 67
timber grain formations
  burr 112, 126–9
  crotch 112
  quilted 112
  rippled 112
  stain marks 112
timber problems
  conversion 61, 62, 64
  end-splitting 60
  pith core 61
  radial cracks 60, 61
  sap wood 61
  sealing 60
  seasoning 62
timbers
  for kitchen use
    beech 68
    box 68
    hornbeam 68
    sycamore 69, 70
  for domestic use
    ash 69
    cherry 60–63, 69
    elm 69
    sycamore 69
    walnut 69
    yew 69

waxes
  beeswax 59
  carnauba 59
  petroleum 59